D1519497

GENTLEMAN JOHNNY
THE LIFE OF GENERAL JOHN BURGOYNE

Gentleman Johnny

THE LIFE OF GENERAL JOHN BURGOYNE

LAURAN   PAINE

LONDON
ROBERT HALE & COMPANY

©Lauran Paine 1973
First published in Great Britain 1973

ISBN 0 7091 3928 4

Robert Hale & Company
63 Old Brompton Road
London SW7

PHOTOSET AND PRINTED BY
REDWOOD PRESS LIMITED, TROWBRIDGE, WILTSHIRE

Contents

Illustrations

ACKNOWLEDGEMENTS

All pictures are reproduced by courtesy
of the Radio Times Hulton Picture Library.

Preface

In the year 1768 when John Burgoyne was governor of Fort William in Scotland, his likeness was created by the eminent portrait painter, Sir Joshua Reynolds, showing Burgoyne in his red coat and looking every inch the capable soldier of George III that in fact he was. That same year the Royal Academy was founded with Sir Joshua as its first President.

Eighteen years earlier in Rome, another portrait painter, Ramsey, also created a likeness in oil of John Burgoyne. It showed a receding chin, coarse lips, lustreless eyes and a general appearance, or attitude, of extreme self-satisfaction.

In 1801, when John Burgoyne had been to the heights and the depths, a delightful engraving was made, showing him face-forward with fine features, a handsome, determined mouth, and a thrusting chin and jaw. Altogether, it would have been easy to associate this flawlessly handsome John Burgoyne with having achieved all the conquests, other than military, attributed to him from his early to his late years.

Another engraving, this one created in the year 1786 as an illustration for John Andrews' *History of the War with America*, a profile view, showed yet another John Burgoyne; this one with a round, strong jaw and chin, and an otherwise unrealistic, general suggestion of chubbiness.

The Ramsey portrait, at Hampton Court Palace for some length of time, the property of a Burgoyne descendant, appears as the most commonly reproduced likeness. Yet the Reynolds portrait is truer. It shows a man who was, at times, pompous and objectionable, and who at other times was a person of feeling, strength of character, and charm. It depicts the real John Burgoyne, the complex man of principles and latitudes whose confidence was formed in civilised Britain, sustained in civilised

Europe, and was shattered in the primaeval chaos of colonial
North America.

Sir Joshua made only an honest effort, nothing more. It was
adequate, and fortunately, it was true, otherwise the engravers
and amateurs who alternately created a *beau sabreur* and a British
bull dog might have successfully distorted this man whose career
was a fair example of the wit, intelligence, background, and
shortcomings, of gentlemen of the times during which John Burgoyne lived.

John Burgoyne was born in London in the year 1722 and died
there on 4th August 1792. He was accomplished as a playwright
and a soldier, and in some ways he was a man who, although
living to the hilt in his own times, belonged to later eras.

He was a loyal conservative who disapproved of the way
common soldiers were treated, and he was a latitudinarian who
bequeathed a great nation several illegitimate progeny.

He was personally known to his monarch, in George's better
days, and he was perspicacious enough to be able to define what
was best among the armies of Europe, and wanted to see every
improvement incorporated into Britain's military system.

Against an orderly foe, French or Spanish or German, he knew
the civilised manoeuvres. Against an armed rabble in America he
faltered because – he was not alone in this – he could not believe
such an untrained, uncouth crowd could, or would, fight.

But Burgoyne's defects, like his triumphs, were demonstrated
by the flux of a changing period; in this he was typical. Unlike
Lord George Germain who planned the Saratoga campaign
where Burgoyne faltered (Germain was safely at home when disaster arrived and it had to be John Burgoyne's sword that was
yielded). It was Burgoyne who was remembered as the victim of
defeat.

Of John Burgoyne's easy morals it can be said he lived in
one of the less moral times, and that he was a virile man
with the appetite of one.

Burgoyne as a politician, to his favour, was not a professional in the sense that he was a professional soldier. He did
very little as Member of Parliament for Midhurst in 1761,
but he accomplished a number of worthwhile exploits in
Portugal and elsewhere as a soldier, which is how he saw
himself. His profession was the army, as it was with hun-

dreds of other British gentlemen of his day, and later.

He liked soldiering and prior to sailing for America, although managing to project an air of indifference if not outright disapproval – the American War was not really popular in Britain – John Burgoyne actually moved heaven and earth to be sent out.

He had defects that hindered some otherwise rather commendable qualities. He allowed gambling and womanising to interfere at times, when it would have been better had he abstained from both. But, also, he deserved of history better than he got, for although he was no Wellington, he was courageous, sensitive, kindly and likable – except when he was being pompous – but even that belonged to an age when pomposity was a requisite not only of soldiers of the rank of colonel or higher, but of well-bred gentlemen.

He was a good strategist if not a brilliant tactician. He commanded well, and at a time when a large percentage of officers were shot in the back while leading troops against an enemy, John Burgoyne was very highly thought of by his soldiers.

As a dramatist, as a soldier, even as a husband, Burgoyne was neither tragic nor comic. The contradictions in his nature were resolved by his essential masculinity. He was every inch a man, and if he was neither a Shakespeare nor a Wellington, it can hardly be held against him. Britain only produced one of each in two thousand years, but the establishment of the bulwarks, as well as the foundations, of empire – yes, *empire* – would have been completely impossible without the John Burgoynes.

ONE

Aspects and Characteristics

The Burgoyne family achieved initial prominence in the year 1387 when Roger Burgoyne was granted property by Lancaster. Subsequent Burgoynes, down to Captain John Burgoyne, father of the man destined to become Lieutenant General John Burgoyne, were all strong and energetic men. Captain John ended his days on the King's bench, saved from penury by this appointment after a lifetime of fashionable profligacy and gambling. His son, with similar predilections, was noted as a gambler, for sartorial elegance, even when in uniform, and also for living beyond his means.

Being a tall, well-proportioned man, solid and sturdy, the son was impressive in either civilian or military attire. Later in life he was called "Handsome Jack", although he was more striking than handsome. He was also called "Gentleman Johnny", and this designation followed him for a good many years, and it came closer to fitting the man than did the other appellation.

John Burgoyne was educated at Westminster. He excelled in history, particularly as it was related to armies and battles; having been destined for the army from earliest youth, and enjoying that prospect, he applied himself to whatever studies were pertinent.

At Westminster, Burgoyne made the acquaintance of Lord Strange, heir to the eleventh Earl of Derby and scion of one of the most prominent and influential families of England. This unique friendship – Burgoyne and Lord Strange had practically nothing in common – brought Burgoyne into close contact with Lord Strange's family, the Stanleys. It lasted until John Burgoyne, a junior officer of the 1st Dragoons and engaged to a young woman named Frances Poole, became interested in Lady Charlotte Stanley, the Earl of Derby's sixth daughter.

This attachment put a strain on the relationship between the Stanleys and John Burgoyne. Only Lord Strange had no objection to his sister marrying his old friend, although his father had some very strenuous objections.

But it was not the Earl of Derby who was amorously involved; it was his daughter. She and John Burgoyne eloped in 1743. Her wedding was in direct violation of the wishes of her father and in consequence he said he never wanted to see her again, and instead of an appropriate dowry sent her only a very small amount of money. With this money Burgoyne bought a captaincy in the 13th Dragoons in the year 1744. He and his lady lived in London during this period, and although Captain Burgoyne lived far too well for his position, and was accumulating gambling debts, his wife's family, influenced by the genuine affection he felt for Charlotte, relented from their earlier hostility.

In 1747, three years after purchasing his captaincy, Burgoyne sold it, overwhelmed with debts, and with his wife went to live near the village of Chantiloup in France, the seat of the august Duc de Choiseul with whom he and his wife formed an enduring friendship.

For the ensuing seven years Burgoyne remained on the continent. He learned the French language. He already knew some Latin. He also had an excellent opportunity to watch Continental politics at close quarters, and to study the condition and composition of Continental armies. He and Charlotte travelled rather extensively, probably on funds furnished by the Stanleys. It was in 1750 that Ramsey, destined to become court painter under George III, painted Burgoyne's portrait in Rome. This was the portrait most cherished by Burgoyne's descendants.

Burgoyne's travels enabled him to examine the various French, Italian, and German military systems as a friendly observer. He made notes on what he saw and was particularly impressed by what was called 'Light Horse', or 'Light Dragoons'. At this time in England there was no such corps; dragoons rode heavy horses and were burdened with defensive and offensive accoutrements. The English conviction, inherited from the days of armoured horsemen, still held that mounted soldiers should be massively outfitted and mounted.

Burgoyne's conclusion was valid. Hungary's Hussars, Russia's

Cossacks, and much earlier, the *la jinetta* horsemen of Spain and Moorish Africa, had proved time and again that there was no match for swift, hard-riding, quick striking, lightly armed mounted troops. It was Burgoyne's feeling that light dragoons would be especially beneficial for the occasional sorties English troops were obliged to make in their frequent continental incursions. He kept this idea to himself during his self-imposed exile and worked out the logistics so that when the time should arrive for an official presentation he would have the facts.

During his seven years on the Continent, John Burgoyne learned a lot, and although he still gambled, and presumably womanised, the two favourite pastimes of his lifetime, he appeared to do less of both than in former times, or perhaps there were fewer opportunities. Meanwhile, elsewhere, events in Europe were moving towards a warlike culmination, the result of two seemingly unrelated conditions. One was the approaching struggle between Britain and France in North America, and the other was the dispute between Prussia and Austria over Silesia.

The juncture occurred, although it was not generally recognised as such, when France went to the aid of Austria, whose claim on Silesia was legitimate, and Britain became the ally of Prussia. Already there was a virtual state of warfare existing in North America between the energetic French and the well-entrenched British. In Europe, it was Britain's design to humble France on the Continent, with Prussia as Britain's ally, and thus win North America on the battlefields of Europe.

There were other British considerations involved. If Prussia's Frederick the Great were vanquished, Britain would be faced by a hostile Continent. It was William Pitt's idea to guard the Prussian's flank against the French until Frederick could crush his enemies in Germany. It was also Pitt's idea to preserve British naval supremacy against France's growing strength at sea. That Pitt was able to accomplish all this, while at the same time being aware of, and sympathetic to, the impatience of the troubled colonial pawns of North America, marked him as one of the most astute Britons of his day, although in the initial stages of the Seven Years War, Britain under Pitt's aegis suffered serious and demoralising reverses.

The British expeditionary force sent to Germany operated under the command of Prince Ferdinand of Brunswick. At home

the strategy of harassing the French coast to prevent a large seg-
ment of the French army from being sent to Germany, fell upon
the shoulders of some capable, and some woefully incapable, British officers. These strikes were not always well-organised or
coordinated, but at least they exerted pressure on the French of
Normandy and Brittany.

In 1756 John Burgoyne rejoined the army as a subordinate
Captain of the 11th Dragoons. His appointment, after so long an
absence, was managed through the influence of Charlotte's
father, but even so Burgoyne was not pleased at the prospect of
now having to serve under men whom he had once commanded,
and apparently he had been assured this would be only a tempor-
ary situation, because on 23rd November 1756, he wrote his
immediate superior, Major Warde, to the effect that, ". . . the
circumstances of serving under so many men whom I had commanded appeared so disagreeable to me, when my friends proposed my entering a second time into the army, that I should not
have suffered any application to be made for me had I not had
good assurance that I should not long continue a captain. . . ."

Evidently the haste with which Burgoyne expected to be promoted atrophied, because he was still a captain in 1758 when he
participated in the Duke of Marlborough's attack upon Cher-
bourg. This joint land–sea operation was notable for the atrocities committed by British troops, and by the destruction of some
French fortifications. It was a fair example of British harassment.

Later, in the same year, Captain Burgoyne participated in the
diversionary strike against St Malo, and in this action Burgoyne
distinguished himself.

The officer in joint command with Admiral Howe of the St
Malo enterprise, Lieutenant General Bligh, was subsequently
categorised by the pithy and gossipy Horace Walpole as "an old
General routed out of some horse armoury in Ireland." Neither
he nor Howe seemed to have felt there would be any danger
connected with the St Malo undertaking. No inland reconnaissance was made before the troops were disembarked upon the
beach at St Cas, and no provision was made for taking the troops
off again although obviously they could not remain many days in
hostile France.

A French deserter came to the British the second day after the
disembarkation and said the Duc d'Aiguillon was hastening up

with a force twice the size of the British contingent. At once word was sent to Admiral Howe, who sent vessels as close to shore as they could get, early the next morning, but General Bligh did nothing about creating a defence. As the invaders clustered on the beach, the Guards and Grenadiers forming a line to the rear, the French were beginning to appear along the heights. As soon as the French started down towards the beach, firing commenced from the frigates. At this time the troops started struggling to reach the vessels. A good many had to wade as far as possible, then swim. Casualties among these men mounted as the French reached the lower ground.

Burgoyne and a companion, seeing a strong detachment of the French swinging into a flanking manoeuvre, quickly sent word to General Bligh. Subsequently, with no orders coming back, Burgoyne and the other junior officer ". . . were obliged to determine upon our own authority," said Burgoyne's later report, "to wheel the divisions we commanded so as to front the enemy."

Confusion ensued when the French poured down upon the beach in great numbers. Some of the British expended all their ammunition and a rout began, everyone trying desperately to swim to a ship. Burgoyne's company made it to safety but all the Grenadiers who had formed the line of defence were either killed or captured, as well as part of the 1st Regiment of Foot; which was abandoned when the ships put to sea.

The St Malo disaster resulted in 400 invaders being captured and about 600 being killed or wounded. In its time it created quite a furore. The soldiers who survived, including Captain Burgoyne, were indignant, and yet for Burgoyne, this opportunity to demonstrate coolness and capability under fire did not go unnoticed. The St Malo affair ensured recognition, and the following year, 1759, when it was decided to raise two regiments of Light Horse, Burgoyne received command of one, the 16th Dragoons. His recruiting posters claimed that enlistees would ". . . be mounted on the finest horses in the world, with superb clothing and the richest accoutrements . . . pay and privileges . . . equal to two guineas a week", while the troopers would be ". . . everywhere respected; your society courted; you are admired by the fair, which, together with the chances of getting switched to a buxom widow, or of brushing with a rich heiress, renders the situation truly enviable and desirable . . . nick in instantly and enlist."

The 16th Dragoons became an exemplary contingent. It at last gave Burgoyne an opportunity to prove his knowledge of light-horse troops. It also gave him an opportunity to demonstrate an aspect of his character that never failed to win him the approbation of the lower ranks. During an age when flogging soldiers, mistreating and maiming them was common throughout Europe, Burgoyne advocated an honour system. He was of the opinion that "An Englishman will not bear beating so well as the foreigners", and wanted less of it in his unit.

He also advocated an occasional show of comradeship between officers and men, at a time when any such thing was unthinkable. He wanted his troops to function by honour and by trust, not by force, fear, and brutality.

If all this was not revolutionary enough, he required that all his officers acquire a competent knowledge of shoeing, caring for, feeding, saddling and bridling their own mounts. It was not advocated that an officer actually do any of these things, enlisted men took charge of this, but a knowledge of how these things should be properly done was required.

John Burgoyne was far in advance of his time as a cavalryman and as an officer. His dragoons had high morale, and although officers seldom agreed with his regulations, they had any number of opportunities to see them vindicated, both on parade at Hounslow Heath or Wimbledon Common (where George III named "Burgoyne's Light Horse" The Queen's Light Dragoons) and in the field against Britain's enemies.

In 1760 Burgoyne's unit was alerted for possible service on the continent under Prince Ferdinand of Brunswick. This came to nothing but the following year when an attack was organised against Belle Isle, Burgoyne joined the expedition as a volunteer and became one of 6000 men of all arms under General Hodgson and Admiral Keppel who were repulsed on 7th April with a loss of 500 men.

A subsequent landing succeeded, the citadel was carried, and on 7th June the British were well established on Belle Isle, where they remained until the Treaty of Paris in 1763, when the island was returned to France.

About this time Burgoyne was elected a member of Parliament

for Midhurst, but events transpired to prevent him from taking his seat. Also about this time, Charlotte Burgoyne, who was always anxious when her husband was away, prevailed upon him to promise that if at all possible, the next time he was sent to serve, she could accompany him.

In the year 1762, with Frederick of Prussia and his British allies victorious on the continent, and with the accession of Peter III removing the Russian threat against the Prussian – British coalition, France and Spain, who had formed their Family Compact the previous year, turned in open hostility upon Portugal. Britain at once declared war on Spain – in January – and the Member of Parliament for the borough of Midhurst received orders to hold himself and his regiment in readiness for overseas service.

The force Britain organised to serve in the Peninsula consisted of slightly more than 7000 troops. Except for a few professional units such as the 16th Light Dragoons, it consisted of fresh levies commanded by inexperienced officers, and the contempt the British ultimately felt for the Portuguese army, was returned to the British by the Germans, all officers, who were already serving in Portugal as a result of Portugal's Prime Minister, Conde de Oeyras, having induced Wilhelm, Count Lippe Buckeburg, to command all the allied forces against Spain.

Lippe Buckeburg's principality of Shaumberg Lippe in northwestern Germany had a population of 30,000 people within a radius of 210 square miles. Ordinarily he might have been categorised as one of the petty princelings of Germany, but Lippe Buckeburg, whose father had been a cousin of England's George II, and who had been born in England, was called by no less an authority than Frederick the Great, "The best artillery officer in the world." He had held a commission in the British army, and more recently had been Prince Ferdinand of Brunswick's chief artillery officer. Prior to arriving in Portugal, he had already served with distinction in any number of campaigns and had been a Field Marshal in Germany. He was only 38 years of age in 1762.

His opinion of the Portuguese army was very low, and justifiably so. Even the soldiers guarding King Joseph's palace in Lisbon begged alms while on duty, and many Portuguese officer's wives took in washing because their husbands were not paid even a subsistence wage. The troops were not so much cowardly as indifferent. They did not view the Spanish invasion as likely to cause them any more misery than they already had, and were reluctant to risk their lives resisting.

When the British transports anchored in the Tagus on 6th May 1762, John Burgoyne was given command of outposts, with a provisional rank of Brigadier General. He and Charlotte found quarters in Lisbon. Lord Loudon, in immediate command of the British expeditionary force, undertook the kind of integration that most British officers found distasteful. The Portuguese levies, when detailed to British units, showed a lack of respect and discipline, not to mention courage in combat, that alienated their Anglo-Saxon allies very quickly.

Brigadier General Burgoyne's Light Horse, one thousand strong, came in for integration, too – not, one may be sure, with the approval of officers or men of this proud unit. Burgoyne's regiment became a brigade, 3000 strong, and discipline was stiffened as much in order to prevent friction as to instill spirit and courage in the Portuguese soldiers.

During this period of adjustment for the Portuguese and their allies, the Franco-Spanish coalition had already invaded Portugal and held a number of towns including Braganza and Mirando. The invading army, although supposed to be largely French, was nine-tenths Spanish. The French did not keep their word and furnished only a small percentage of the number of troops they had promised, but French officers served in large numbers.

The Spanish commander, the Marquis de Saria, had 42,000 men and nearly a hundred cannon. A subordinate 'Spanish' officer, General O'Reilly, was pressing vigorously towards Oporto with another column. Altogether, by July, when Lippe Buckeburg got his heterogenous and vastly inferior army on the move, the invaders were already threatening an approach to Lisbon itself, with their oncoming three columns.

Lippe Buckeburg's strategy was to strike the advancing columns separately, before they reached flat country and before they converged.

The enemy's third column was lying near the fortified city of Valentia d'Alcantara. Here, aside from a Spanish supply depot, there was also a train of artillery and a great store of ammunition. Lippe Buckeburg's orders to General Burgoyne were to hasten to Valentia d'Alcantara and prevent the Spaniards from marching

towards a juncture with the other invading columns.
If possible Burgoyne was to destroy the ammunition at Valentia d'Alcantara while Lippe Buckeburg advanced against the neighbouring Spanish outposts at Selvorino and St Vincent, and cut the Spaniards off from communication and reinforcements.

Burgoyne struck out quickly with his entire brigade. By a forced march he was able to cross the Castel de Vida mountains well ahead of any intelligence that might have warned the Spaniards of his coming, but his haste also cost him the support of two elements of Portuguese infantry that were supposed to aid him at Valentia d'Alcantara, and beyond. In his own words what followed happened in this way:

According to my intelligence I was to find the town situated in a plain: the principal entrance there, one on the Pitteranha Road (which was that I marched), to the east; one on the great road to Alcantara, on the west; and one towards the mountains, on the south; on the north, only some small inlets. . . . Lord Pulteney with the British grenadiers was ordered to form the attack on the Pitteranha Road. . . . The Portuguese irregulars were to take post opposite the entrance on the side of the mountains, and endeavour to make themselves masters of some houses of the entrance of the town on that side. The English Light Dragoons were, upon their arrival in the plain, to form on the north side, from whence Colonel Somerville had orders to detach a captain's command on the road to St Vincent, which were the only passages by which the enemy could retreat, or from which he could receive succour. . . . My idea was to attack on three sides at once; and I had given the Alcantara side to the Portuguese . . . to reserve the English for a rush into the town, in case I should find we were discovered. . . . I perceived with much dissatisfaction that my guides had greatly deceived me . . . that the sun would be risen before the foot could possibly reach the town: I thought it therefore expedient to lay aside entirely my first disposition, and carry forward the light dragoons, who by a brisk gallop might possibly still effect a surprise, or at worst stop up the avenues. I accordingly went on with that corps at three-quarters speed without molestation, and the advanced guard, consisting of forty men, led by Lieutenant Lewis, finding the entrance clear, pushed into the town sword in hand.

The guards in the square were all killed or made prisoner, before they could use their arms, and the end of the streets were possessed with very little resistance. . . . A few desperate parties attempted an attack, but all perished or were taken. The only firing that remained was in long shots from windows, which did not continue long after the grenadiers came up. I was obliged to treat the people who persisted in it without quarter and at last got some priests, whom I forced through the town, to declare that the town should be set afire to, at the four corners, unless all doors and windows were instantly thrown open. Before they had proceeded down one street, the people had seen their error and all was quiet. . . . I brought off prisoners, Major General Don Michael de Irunibeni and Kalanca, and his aide-de-camp, one colonel and his adjutant, two captains, seventeen subalterns, and fifty-nine privates. There were taken and brought off besides three colours, and a large quantity of arms, and a good many more, together with ammunition, destroyed. . . .

TWO

The Years of Peace

King Joseph of Portugal was so elated at Burgoyne's success that he presented him with a letter of commendation and a diamond ring, and although Lippe Buckeburg also commended Burgoyne, the action at Valentia d'Alcantara while certainly impressive, was not decisive as far as the war went. The conflict dragged on through a hot summer, and during this time Burgoyne busied himself with trying to procure for himself the rank of full colonel. He was unsuccessful, largely, so he was informed, because of the large number of lieutenant colonels whose ranks were superior to his.

On 5th October, Burgoyne, whose brigade had been watching the Spaniards slowly advance, forcing Lippe Buckeburg to retreat, ordered Colonel Charles Lee to cross the Tagus with a detachment of 250 British grenadiers and 50 Light Dragoons and strike the Spanish garrison at Villa Velha. The major force had been withdrawn from Villa Velha to chase Lord Loudon, who was covering the withdrawal of a Portuguese brigade under Conde San Jago, that had been seriously mauled in combat.

Lee was a remarkable man. He managed to infiltrate the Villa Velha encampment undetected and burst upon the astonished Spaniards at bayonet-point. When the Spaniards attempted to rally, Colonel Lee at the head of his little force "pursued them upon a brisk run", out of their camp inflicting great loss. He spiked six cannon, destroyed Spanish magazines, brought off a great number of pack animals, all at the trifling cost of a few casualties, and so demoralised the Spaniards they would not move until reinforcements had been sent to them.

Burgoyne came in for much of the credit for this strike, as senior commander – and also because Charles Lee was an unpopular, irascible, sarcastic, belligerent man. Lee's courage was legendary. His whole life was soldiering. He despised Britain's monarch, George III under whom he served. He had been an ensign at the age of 16, a captain at 24, a major at 30, and in 1772 a brevet lieutenant colonel. He served with distinction under Abercromby and Amherst in North America during the French and Indian War, and after the event at Villa Velha, was presented with testimonials of good conduct and bravery by both Lippe Buckeburg and the King of Portugal. Later, the thin, nervous, brooding Lee served as a major-general in the Polish army, fought the Turks for the Russians in 1769, and in 1773 he was back in North America again, but as an avowed enemy of George III. He was second in seniority under George Washington, as a United States major general.

The campaign in Portugal ended when the embattled British and Portuguese were able to avoid being overwhelmed until the rainy season arrived, and before the Spaniards could renew hostilities, the Treaty of Paris, which was concluded early in 1763, ended the Seven Years War.

Lieutenant Colonel Burgoyne, whose exploits had captured the popular imagination in Britain, embarked for home with his troops late in the year 1763. Whether he or his men were aware of it or not, William Pitt's masterful strategy had worked to the letter. Canada belonged to Britain, French sea-might had been eclipsed, India was saved for the empire, through the heroic efforts of Robert Clive, and although the impetuous and mettlesome North American colonists were still not appeased, at least, with French *provocateurs* removed from their midst, it was possible that some kind of accommodation might prevail.

Britain, at the conclusion of the Seven Years War, was held in higher esteem throughout the world than ever before. She had acquired additional French possessions in both West Africa and in the West Indian archipelago, her claim to empire was great and unchallenged. The Irish were quiet, North America, though soon to smoulder, was not in any way organised in its dissension in 1763, and the troublesome French had been humbled both in Europe and in Canada.

George III, who had come to the throne in 1760, successor to his German grandfather, was able to profit from peace, the first British monarch to have that opportunity since the accession of

Queen Anne at the beginning of the century. This was fortunate
since the National Debt had grown from 14 million in 1702, on
Queen Anne's accession, to 130 million in 1762. This was largely
the result of endless warfare, to which the Seven Years War was
certainly no exception.

That particular war, in which William Pitt gambled for, and
won, so much, cost Britain no less·than 112 millions, most of
which was raised by direct taxation. At the conclusion of this
conflict, Britain, whose population did not exceed seven and a
half million people at the beginning of George III's reign (but by
the end of it had doubled its population) was subsidising no less
than 60,000 foreign soldiers, and was otherwise supporting allies
from Germany to Portugal.

Losses during the Seven Years War, for such a small population, were equally impressive. Among seamen and marines alone,
184,893 men perished. In other areas the losses were correspond-
ingly great.

But peace arrived, and with it some prospects for its continuance, and in 1763 Colonel Burgoyne – finally confirmed at this
rank on 18th March 1763 – took his seat in the House of Commons where he and his 16th Dragoons, now known officially as
the Queen's Light Dragoons, received the thanks of Parliament
for their gallantry in Portugal.

For the ensuing twelve years, or for as long as there was peace,
Colonel Burgoyne had the leisure to actively participate in politics, and to make a trip over the continental battlefields of the
recent war, perhaps with a view towards writing a military
chronology of what had transpired. Also at this time he undertook some of the literary compositions that made him notable in
a modest way·as an author and playwright.

He and Charlotte were welcomed at court, and Burgoyne was
known to William Pitt – Lord Chatham – whose haughtiness did
not allow him to visit or exchange correspondence with many
army colonels. But he often did both with John Burgoyne.

After Burgoyne's visit to the continent in 1765, he sent Lord
Chatham a somewhat voluminous but excellent synopsis of his
observations of the various military situations in Germany and
France, and in return received the following letter:

Monday, December 14, 1766

Dear Sir, – I will not attempt to tell you how much pleasure and how much instruction I have received from the perusal of the Observations, &c., which you was so good to send me. It would not be less difficult for me to describe the sensations which the honour of the letter accompanying the Observations have filled me with. Allow me to offer, in one hasty line, more real acknowledgements than the longest letter could contain; and to assure you that I count the minutes while indispensable business deprives me of the pleasure of seeing you. If Wednesday morning next at eleven should suit your convenience, I shall be extremely happy in the honour of seeing you at that time.

I am, with the truest esteem and most distinguished consideration,

Dear Sir,

Your most faithful

and most obedient, humble servant,

Chatham.

It did no harm to have the active support of the Stanley family in most of Colonel Burgoyne's various undertakings, political, military, and civil, and when Charlotte's father died leaving her £25,000 outright and an annuity of £400, the Burgoyne fortunes were considerably strengthened. An additional cause for gratification arrived in the form of an appointment from the King as commandant of Fort William in Scotland, a position of trust and responsibility usually conferred only upon officers of the rank of general. This occurred in the year 1768.

The Fort William appointment carried with it considerable prestige and remuneration. It also implied that the King, and others who were responsible for the appointment, considered Colonel Burgoyne an officer worthy of promotion.

The Burgoynes at long last had no need to avoid society because they could not afford the cost. They were a handsome couple and moved in elegant circles. Presumably the colonel gambled and flirted, as he usually did, but he was uniquely loyal to Charlotte, if not always faithful to her, and whatever gambling debts he may have incurred at this time were either promptly taken care of or were not exorbitant, because there was no scandal. His range of friends included a great number of influential people, and except for one fiery interlude, the General Election of 1768, that year passed well for the colonel and his lady.

John Burgoyne and Sir Henry Hoghton were nominated to run for Parliament for the borough of Preston, a place under the influence of the Stanley family. The Tories of Preston put up two men of their choice in opposition, Sir Frank Standish and Sir Peter Leicester, and what should have been a commonplace election gradually became a total brawl. Burgoyne, Hoghton and the Whigs met force with force. When Tory troublemakers attempted coercion, the Whigs retaliated with a vengeance. Voters were intimidated, threatened and beaten.

When the votes were ultimately cast and counted it appeared that Burgoyne and Hoghton had won with a comfortable margin, but the Tory supporters of Leicester and Standish declared *their* men had won because the Whigs had indulged in fraud.

The result of this fierce deadlock was a petition to the House of Commons, which confirmed the election of Burgoyne and Hoghton. Riots broke out in Preston, there was some bloodshed, and both Whigs and Tories had armed bands roaming the countryside. When the trouble subsided, Burgoyne, among others, was indicted for having encouraged his supporters in their violence. He appeared in April 1769 before Justice Yates and admitted under questioning that he had gone to the polling place with a pistol in each hand because he expected to be attacked, and although he implied that which was general knowledge, that the Tories had been armed by the Mayor from a local arsenal, Burgoyne was found guilty. He was fined one thousand pounds, and narrowly escaped being sentenced to jail, which was the fate of some of the others charged with him.

For better or for worse, John Burgoyne represented the borough of Preston until 1792, the year of his death.

Subsequent to being fined, an anonymous writer calling himself "Junius" said that the Duke of Grafton had given Colonel Burgoyne £3,500 "to reward him, I presume, for the decency of his deportment at Preston . . . " then went on to attack Burgoyne as a gambler who took advantage of others, and called him a man "not very conspicuous in his profession" of arms, and Burgoyne reacted in anger, but since no one ever actually proved who "Junius" was, there was no duel, nor even any exchange of words.

As Member of Parliament for Preston, Burgoyne, with the

right of free and independent speech, was initially a friend of the
ministry, with his chief concerns being the war office and foreign
policy, but his most notable speeches were against the government in the Falkland Islands affair in 1771, and on the government of India in 1772. His India motion demonstrated his ability
as a statesman, and in this motion for a select committee, he
advocated the policy that was subsequently adopted by Pitt and
Fox, that some measure of control be instituted over the func-
tions of the East India Company.

When the Select Committee reported on 3rd May 1773, Burgoyne used its findings as the basis for a fierce attack upon Lord
Clive, causing his condemnation by the House of Commons
although a defender of Clive was able to prevent a vote for
impeachment.

Burgoyne's independence did not endear him to the King,
who was very sensitive about opposition of any kind, But when
Burgoyne voted for the Royal Marriage Act, His Majesty was
prepared to forgive what he considered Burgoyne's earlier trans-
gressions. He told Lord North in a letter that had Burgoyne
failed to vote as he did on this issue ". . . I should have felt myself
obliged to name a new Governor for Fort William." The King
also told Lord Bute that "his passions were similar to those of
other young men," something no-one doubted since His Majesty
was rumoured to have married a young Quakeress, Hannah
Lightfoot, and was known to be very fond of Lady Sarah
Lennox, among others.

THREE

Towards the Year 1775

In 1770 when there was more than a rumour of dissension in North America, King George addressed the Members of Parliament on 19th January at their initial session by informing them that ". . . the distemper among the horned cattle has lately broken out in this kingdom", and scarcely mentioned the American colonies at all. Subsequently, a number of deriders, both at home and overseas, called His Majesty "Farmer George".

This name appeared to particularly please the King's detractors in America, where he was villainised as a tyrant, a stubborn German, and a person whose opinionated notions could not be confirmed by an appeal to logic.

There was enough truth in the charge to merit its acceptance. His Majesty, taught by his mother, encouraged by Lord Bute, and confirmed in his general oppositions by Lord North (who had headed the government for five years by 1775) was unshakable in his convictions concerning the royal prerogatives and arbitrary rule.

Nor did conditions prior to the year 1775 suggest that Farmer George might at best be mistaken, and at worst be following an outmoded variety of Divine Right. For two decades after the Ministry of the elder Pitt, opposition was weak, and when Lord North's premiership (1770–1782) proved itself not very concerned or at best "a mere instrument of the royal will", His Majesty was able to resume the practice of royal patronage, which further strengthened his position as sole arbiter.

Perhaps, as Trevelyan has noted, none of this would have succeeded "if Cabinet government had then rested on democracy instead of an aristocracy, on opinion instead of on 'management' ". But the fact was that it *did* succeed, and at a time

when overseas in the colonies an entirely antithetical point of
view was sweeping the settlements from New England to the
Carolinas. The earlier view that when the French had been vanquished a closer relationship between crown and colonies would
exist evolved into something altogether different. With the need
for cohesiveness against the common enemy removed, the colonists decided not to be conciliatory towards the crown.

Events went from bad to worse. On both sides of the Atlantic
there were sceptics and firebrands, but in Britain there was a
common belief that the colonists would not, and could not, fight.
They had not distinguished themselves during the French and
Indian War and upon a number of occasions they had been
routed on their various frontiers. When cooperation between
colonies had been desirable, the colonists had demonstrated an in-
ability to agree. They appeared more irascible than courageous.

Taxation was a sore issue. So was George Grenville's outright
anti-Americanism, as well as his proposal that the colonists pay
about one-third of the £360,000 it would cost to maintain ten
thousand British soldiers in North America, ostensibly to protect
American frontiers, but claimed by the colonists to be a means
for oppressing them.

Anti-Americanism also motivated the Declaratory Act which
followed repeal of the very unpopular Stamp Act, but the colonists were so pleased over the withdrawal of the latter enactment,
which they were sure had been repealed as a result of their
clamour, that they were slow to realise that the Declaratory Act
was worse. It stated that the King and Parliament had "full
power and authority" to legislate for the colonies "in all cases
whatsoever".

Between the repeal of the first enactment, and the realisation of
the purpose of the other, there were considerable reiterations of
loyalty. Very probably at this time only a little tact would have
dispelled most of the discord, but there were three unfortunate
circumstances that intervened. One was King George's driving
ambition for unrestrained personal power, which he saw questioned by "seditious" colonials, towards whom he was both
ignorant and prejudiced. The second was William Pitt's (now
Earl of Chatham) prolonged siege of gout and melancholia,
which robbed the ministry of its only outstanding leader at a
time when Farmer George was using patronage to increase the

strength and number of the "King's Friends" in Parliament, while the third was that the Chancellor of the Exchequer and former Lord-Lieutenant of Ireland, Charles Townshend, who was responsible for finding new sources of revenue, was distinctly hostile to the colonies and wasted no time in taking advantage of his position to translate his feelings into deeds. One of Townshend's acts was the Duty Act, which imposed fresh taxes on tea, paper, glass, lead and painters' colours entering the colonies. Coinciding with a revelation of the meaning of the Declaratory Act, this started the furor all over again. Charles Townshend died shortly afterwards and amiable, easy-going Lord North spent the next three years attempting to enforce the unpopular Townshend Acts.

Samuel Adams of Massachusetts led colonial resistance to the vexatious Townshend Acts. He saw them as a threat to all freedom and, with others, said as much in an atmosphere that had been growing increasingly abusive towards the crown for months. Then, on the day that Lord North moved for repeal, 5th March 1770, a crowd of jeering Bostonians drove a detachment of British soldiers to distraction; the soldiers fired and five Americans lay dead. John Adams, a young lawyer and a distant relation of Samual Adams, acted as counsel for the soldiers.

This, the so-called "Boston Massacre", was an ideal *causus belli*, but as a matter of fact, although the bitterness it engendered did not diminish in some areas, the news that the Townshend duties had been repealed tended to aid in the restoration of order. Many of the retaliatory non-importation agreements made by the colonials, which bound them not to buy anything with tax stamps attached, or that came from England, were rescinded. Tact alone could not have prevailed this time, and it is improbable that even enduring goodwill might have achieved peace, for by now a band of lusty radicals had burned a British revenue cutter, the *Gaspee*, on the Rhode Island coast; Samuel Adams was busy organising a group of colonial leaders to watch affairs with a view towards fostering dissention and sedition again, and moreover there were groups of active dissidents throughout the colonies to whom goodwill on the part of the crown would have meant nothing.

Then, in May 1773, the British government made a very spectacular blunder. It tried to aid the East India Company which had a surplus of tea on hand, by agreeing to remit the twelve pence a pound duty charged on tea imported into Britain so that the tea could be trans-shipped to America, where it would be subject to a threepence duty. Actually, if the price of tea had been the issue, there probably would have been little difficulty, because this imported tea sold more cheaply than smuggled tea. But this was construed in a different light — taxation, again, without representation — and at Boston the tea was hurled into the sea, while ships similarly laden at New York and Philadelphia were not permitted to unload, and returned to England with their cargoes.

Britons regarded the "Boston Tea Party" as an outrage. Seizure of the tea was an attack upon the private property of a British company. In 1774 Parliament, with public approval, passed what the Americans called the "Intolerable Acts". The Boston Port Act ordered that the port of Boston be closed to all commerce until the destroyed tea had been paid for. The Massachusetts Government Act reformed the rather liberal colonial status of that colony's government, increasing the power of the Royal Governor, suppressing town meetings, making some elective offices appointive, and reducing Massachusetts to little more than a royal dependency.

Another "Intolerable Act" was the Act for the Impartial Administration of Justice, which enabled royal officials accused of capital crimes in Massachusetts to return to England for trial. The Quartering Act, applicable to other colonies as well as Massachusetts, authorised royal governors to requisition whatever buildings they might need for the housing of troops.

Finally, there was the Quebec Act, and while this not only extended the boundaries of Canada to include the territory north of the Ohio River and east of the Mississippi, in disregard of the land claims of the seaboard colonies, the Quebec Act also confirmed Catholicism in French Canada at a time when Catholicism was healthily detested not only in Britain itself, but in all the New England colonies as well.

These measures could not have aroused colonial indignation any better if they had been designed for that purpose, not only in Massachusetts but elsewhere. When the royal governor, General Thomas Gage, appeared in Boston to enforce the acts with four regiments of regulars, apprehension became rife in the other colonies lest they suffer the same suppression of liberties that Parliament had decreed for Massachusetts.

The Quebec Act not only blocked the westward expansion of the colonies that had, or thought they had, claims to western lands, but even more ominous, it threatened the English-speaking colonies with an end to self-government, a limitation on the colonists' rights as Britons, and the encouragement of Roman Catholicism as a counter-weight to New England Puritanism.

In relation to the offences committed, the reprisals of the crown were very drastic. The committees of correspondence founded by Samuel Adams began to function defiantly and angrily. Massachusetts was assured of sympathy and support from the radical elements throughout the colonies. A Virginia resolution called upon all the colonies to send delegates to a Continental Congress in Philadelphia. Serious trouble was in the making.

The years of difficulty and antagonism had split colonial society into two well-defined categories. That the British monarch and his government had dealt harshly with the colonies was generally conceded, but opinions were divergent about colonial response. The radicals such as Tom Paine, Samuel Adams, Patrick Henry and many others, were determined never to yield to force and suppression. They proposed to regain all their rights as Americans, and to acquire new ones if possible, and if necessary they would fight.

The conservatives, who saw more clearly the advantages to be derived from British trade and protection, favoured conciliation, and even after the fighting began, those people still maintained their feeling that America could profit most from being part of the empire. To yield a few rights in exchange for the benefits arising from favoured status within the empire seemed to the conservatives a worthwhile exchange. Unfortunately, there were never as many conservatives as there were lower and middle-class radicals. But, too, particularly among the southern colonies, there were factions of wealthy and aristocratic colonists whose outrage over British policy and threats, drove them to make common cause with the radicals.

But the issue was not that clearly defined, even up to 4th September 1774 when the first Continental Congress convened in Philadelphia. Many thoughtful Americans were more concerned

with who was to rule in the colonies than they were with home
rule. In other words, like most Carolina colonials, they were not
convinced that home rule or independence was preferable to
some kind of royal administration at the top with colonial administration at the lower levels, all within some kind of a commonwealth.

The issues facing America were thorny. There was unanimity
only among the firebrands who had little to lose, being by and
large men of no substance. The conservatives were a minority in
Philadelphia, where 56 delegates met, representing every colony
but Georgia, and worse, the conservatives were splintered by different views even on their own issues.

Joseph Galloway of Pennsylvania proposed a compromise plan
that would have provided for a council of delegates to deal with
all differences between crown and colonies, subject to the veto of
a president-general appointed by the crown, and although this
could hardly have pleased the radical separatists, its adoption was
defeated by only one vote.

The radicals then offered their own plan, a Declaration of
Rights and Grievances, which re-stated the American case against
taxation without representation, and demanded repeal of the
Intolerable Acts. The delegates then created a "Continental
Association" whose purpose was to re-instate and enforce the old
embargoes against the importation of any British "goods, wares,
or merchandise whatsoever", with local committees of enforcement in every colony.

These acts were basically hostile and revolutionary. Without
any authority whatever, and in fact in clear and open defiance of
the crown, that first Continental Congress had passed a law and
had provided the means for its enforcement as though America
were a sovereign nation.

This was viewed throughout the colonies as proof that the
colonials were in deadly earnest, but there were still only a few
voices raised for separation and independence.

The Association for non-importation was a success, but of
course non-importation was an old weapon among the colonists; they knew how, for example, to make fox-berry tea as a
(poor) substitute for India tea. It was a simple step from this to
propose that home industries be improvised to make the things
that non-importation kept out of the homes and stores of

Colonial America, and still another step was taken which would diminish dependence on Britain.

Finally, as a further precaution against oppression, militia companies were formed, munitions were acquired and stored, and homespun 'soldiers' drilled on the village greens. All of these events had the effect upon British opinion that the Americans had rather thought they might, and if the division was noticeable in the colonies, it was equally so in Britain. The municipality of London, for example presented its "humble address" deprecating the employment of force against the colonists, and His Majesty reacted with anger and obstinacy.

Edmund Burke, Chatham and Charles Fox were three voices raised in opposition to fresh oppression. It was asked that the Intolerable Acts be repealed. British merchants, losing heavily as a result of the American boycotts – the non-importation agreements – petitioned Parliament to conciliate the colonies, but this time the ministry, strongly supported by an indignant and autocratic monarch – who, up until now, had been jealous of his government's power – refused to yield and voted instead to send more troops to America.

The fatal step thus taken did not necessarily ensure conflict, which was already possible in America where Britain-baiting as a popular pastime was becoming increasingly popular, but it *did* ensure that Britain was shortly to embark upon a course of action that ultimately saw her faced by half the world in armed hostility. Before the American Rebellion ended the Franco-Spanish Family Compact was renewed to challenge Britain at sea, and eventually even on land in America. Elsewhere, Holland, Russia, and Britain's former ally Prussia, plus the Scandinavian Powers, formed a côterie of naval and diplomatic nations opposed to Britain's course, and for the first – and last – time in Irish history Protestants and Catholics stood united against the king and the British system. Against this kind of opposition, much of it openly hostile, Britain would have been amply occupied, without also having to wage a foreign war, but men like Sir Gilbert Eliott (formerly commander of the 15th Light Dragoons and a friend of John Burgoyne's when both had been colonels) who successfully defended Gibraltar against France and Spain, and Warren Hastings who saved India for the crown, helped salvage what a stubborn and vindictive monarch and a number of short-sighted and untalented men like Lord North very nearly lost.

The belief that Americans would not fight persisted, too. But not everyone shared that feeling. David Hartley (the younger) who would subsequently face Benjamin Franklin in the discussions that led to the Peace Treaty in 1783, made a spirited speech in the House of Commons in the last week of March 1775, in which he said: "Everything is asserted about America to serve the present turn without the least regard for truth. I would have these matters fairly sifted out." For those who belittled colonial courage Hartley said:

> General Monkton took . . . Nova Scotia with 1,500 provincial troops and about 200 regulars. Sir William Johnson in the other part of America changed the face of the war to success, with a provincial army . . . Nor did they [the Americans] stint their services to North America; they followed the British arms out of their continent to Havannah and Martinique. . . . They were not grudging of their exertions . . . but as members of the common cause, [served to] . . . the glory of this country! . . . they took Louisburg [in 1745] from the French, singlehanded, without any European assistance; as mettled an enterprise as any in our history! An everlasting memorial of the zeal, courage and perseverance of the troops of New England. . . . Whenever Great Britain has declared war, they have taken their part. They were engaged in King William's War and Queen Anne's War, even in their infancy. They conquered Nova Scotia, which, from that time has always belonged to Great Britain. . . . They have been . . . ever foremost to partake of honour and danger with the mother country. Well, Sir, what have we done for them? Have we conquered the country for them from the Indians? Have we cleared it? Have we made it habitable? What have we done for them? I believe precisely nothing at all, but just keeping watch and ward over their trade, that they should receive nothing but from ourselves, and at out own price.

The Duke of Grafton warned the King against additional coercive measures in 1775, and his resignation led to reconstruction of the Cabinet resulting in the appointment of Lord George Germain – who was once court-martialled for cowardice in combat – as American Secretary. Germain was to prove as compliant a tool of Farmer George as was Lord North.

Lord Sandwich was sure the Americans would not stand up to

British regulars, while the Duke of Gloucester favoured giving up the colonies altogether. John Burgoyne, with a low view of almost all foreigners as soldiers, thought that what America needed was a brisk chastisement, while "Junius" was of the opinion that while the government certainly had the *right* to dominate the American colonies, he deplored the fact that the government would do so.

Lord North, to avoid being replaced, humoured His Majesty, and no one, it seems, cared to remind the King that Great Britain aside from being in an excellent way of antagonising half the world, was staggering under a crippling debt of £148,000,000, before any additional war-like expenses were incurred at all.

In George III's view, and justifiably, Britain had never been greater, more prosperous, more respected, than up until the year 1775. It was inconceivable to His Majesty that loyal Englishmen would not favour his plan of unyielding opposition to colonial demands, but many Englishmen did oppose him, and they were men of national renown such as Captain James Wilson, Member of Parliament and officer of Marines who requested ". . . leave to lay down his commission, as he cannot . . . consistently with his conscience serve in the present dispute against the Americans."

When His Majesty offered Jeffrey Amherst supreme command in America, he declined to serve. Lord Chatham directed his son, Lord Pitt, aide to Sir Guy Carleton, Governor of Canada, to resign his commission, and a man named John Horne ended up being fined £200 and being imprisoned for one year as a result of inducing the "Constitutional Society of Cornhill" to contribute £100 for ". . . the relief of the widows and orphans MURDERED by the KING's troops . . . in the Province of Massachusetts."

Lord Chesterfield made a wry comment. He had not, he said, ever seen "a forward child mended by whipping; and I would not have the Mother Country become a step-mother," but it was John Burgoyne's comment that best summed up the view, not of the King, who was far more truculent, but the view of many Members of Parliament whose patience had been exhausted by colonial defiance in the form of demands rather than requests. "I look upon America as our child, which we have already spoilt by too much indulgence."

If Burgoyne had taken his adverse stand with a view towards winning the King's approval he could not have chosen a better way, for Admiral Keppel had said he would not ". . . draw his sword . . ." against the Americans, and the renowned soldier, Ralph Abercromby took a similar stand, while the Earl of Effingham resigned his commission on the grounds that he could not, "without reproach from [his] own conscience consent to bear arms against my fellow-subjects in America in what, to my discernment, is not a clear cause."

But there was also some ambiguity. Sir William Howe, who was to succeed inept General Gage in America, although following the popular trend among superior officers and telling his Nottingham constituents that he would refuse if offered the command in America, when the appointment arrived, managed to achieve a very swift and salutary accommodation with his conscience.

John Burgoyne, on the other hand, never entertained a doubt about where his duty lay, and although his bellicose stand was not universally popular, he had the courage to maintain it in the face of some rather strong and noisy opposition.

FOUR

To North America

Among men in high places who epitomised the division in
Britain were George III and Lord Chatham. The former said,
"Every means of distressing America must meet with my concur-
rence," and Chatham, although no longer able to influence the
government, and called a "trumpet of sedition" for his views,
said, "I trust that the minds of men are more than beginning to
change on this subject so little understood, and that it will be impossible for free men in England to wish to see three million
slaves in America."

But, divided though Britons were, and unpopular as this kind
of a conflict always has been in the English-speaking world,
when the fighting commenced His Majesty's government was
ably supported by the majority of Britons. However, as time
passed, it became increasingly difficult to recruit soldiers and
seamen in Britain with the result that Germans were hired and
Indians were employed, two additional causes for the unyielding
opposition of the colonists.

Another cause for colonial anger was the steady stream of loyal
comment coming out of England. Samuel Johnson wrote with an
infuriating superiority that "We have always protected the
Americans; we may therefore subject them to government."
And: "Liberty is to the lowest rank of every nation little more
than the choice of working or starving." Johnson's avowal to
Boswell that "all foreigners are fools," was consistent with his
bigotry, and if others could shrug him off, the Americans could
not, because after 1775 they found very little about the mother
country to be indifferent about.

Even the gentle Hertfordshire poet William Cowper, who
abhorred war and violence, wrote that it was the King's ". . .

duty he owes to himself and his people . . . as a trustee, deriving his interest from God . . ." to defend his kingly prerogatives with the sword.

Hardly a voice was raised as early as 1775 in support of a *peaceful* separation betwèen Britain and America, although a little later, in 1777, the Honourable Charles Fox said that sooner than continue this wretched war he would treat with the Americans as allies, and he made another pronouncement that demonstrated personal courage when he said that he could not consent to the bloody consequences of so silly a contest, about so silly an object, conducted in the silliest manner that history or observation had ever furnished an instance of, and from which we were likely to derive nothing but poverty, disgrace, defeat and ruin."

The primary reason no-one advocated peaceful disunion was because even men such as Chatham actually believed that, regardless of how they felt concerning actual war with the colonists, the loss of Britain's American colonies would mean the end of the empire and the ruin of England. That no such condition was discernible in 1775 or 1777 did not alter conviction in high places, where it was held that colonies existed largely to contribute to the wealth and well-being of the mother-country. The same Englishmen who would have most clamorously and strenuously resisted any abrogation of their own freedom, demonstrated very well how blind they could be to their own defects by refusing the same liberties to the Americans, and no one, not even those who really hoped it might happen, believed the most powerful nation of Europe, could be beaten in a war by a scattering of frontiersmen, half their number in population, fit only to fight Indians, whose noise had always seemed more formidable than their actions. Government opinion,- happily or otherwise, was reflected in a remark made in the House of Commons in May 1774, when the Massachusetts Bill was up for discussion: "Resist, and we will cut your throats – acquiesce, and we will tax you."

That Continental Congress that met in Philadelphia in 1774 and assumed the prerogatives of a sovereign nation, aroused such indignation in Britain that it was decided to strengthen Crown forces in America, at that time numbering less than 10,000 men under General Thomas Gage, which was an excellent idea because in Boston alone, General Gage lost 500 regulars through desertion, a trouble that plagued him constantly.

Parliament was sharply divided about sending additional troops to America at a time when every American was extremely sensitive on this issue, but His Majesty was adamant and his "friends" supported him, thus, in 1775 the preparations were undertaken.

In May 1772 John Burgoyne, progressing militarily better in peacetime than in war, was confirmed a Major General. He remained a cavalryman, commander of the 16th or the Queen's Own Dragoons. It might be said that John Burgoyne in Portugal had really achieved some kind of personal apex, and like his nation, shone best at that time, in an environment that seemed particularly compatible to his capabilities which is not to say that he could not, in time, have mastered the American ethos, but there lay the trouble – he did not get the time. But, with a war-like atmosphere being revived in Britain, and with much doubt about which, if any, of the tried and seasoned generals might be willing to go out to the colonies, John Burgoyne, while affecting indifference, encouraged the opinion that he would accept an offer if it were made. Because he was known to favour the King's views, the right of Imperial prerogatives in colonial policy, and also because he was now an officer of exemplary rank, he was appointed. He accepted, as did Lord Cornwallis. Burgoyne consistently held a view that force was justified, but Cornwallis disagreed with government policy and favoured the American cause in Parliament, while at the same time soliciting an American command. When he got it, like William Howe, Cornwallis managed a swift and convenient accommodation with his science, and by some unique rationalisation of his own changed practically overnight from a champion of justice to the King's general.

Military reinforcements, plus three British major generals, William Howe (the admiral's brother), Henry Clinton and John Burgoyne, were sent to America, subordinate to General Gage, in 1775. Of the three officers Burgoyne's commission was most recent, making him a junior in seniority. From this fact it has been inferred he saw slight chance of advancement, another consideration supposedly contributing to his reluctance to go to America, but as a matter of fact the surest way for him to win advancement from now on would be in warfare, and he would have been well aware of this.

He did, however, have one valid reason for wishing he might remain in England: Charlotte. "To separate for a length of time, perhaps forever, from the tenderest, the faithfullest, the most amiable companion and friend that ever a man was blessed with . . . added severely to my anxieties." This time there was no plan for the General's lady to accompany him, although, despite the prevailing contrary views in Britain, North America was more likely to be enjoyed by an officer's wife in 1775, than Portugal had been in 1762.

If Burgoyne had any other reservations they must have arisen from the fact that prior to being sent to America none of the three major generals were "called before the Cabinet, or by some other method consulted upon a plan of measures." It was distressing, to say the least, to be sent overseas like so many levies, but that was what happened.

En route Burgoyne no doubt heard from William Howe the very low opinion Howe had of Thomas Gage. He may also have heard from Howe, who could be garrulously disagreeable for great lengths of time, that he had not wanted to go to America, where Bostonians had erected a monument to Brigadier General Lord Howe, killed at Ticonderoga, and his descendant was conscious of an "obligation".

In April 1775, General Burgoyne wrote a rather lengthy letter to be delivered to the King in the event of his death while on active service in America. It began: "Sire: – Whenever this letter shall be delivered to your Majesty, the writer of it will be no more . . ." and stated as its purpose "to recommend to your royal protection Lady Charlotte Burgoyne, who at my death will have to combat the severest calamities of life – a weak frame of body, very narrow circumstances, and a heart replete with those agonies which follow the loss of an object it has long held most dear. . . ." There was no need to deliver this letter. Charlotte predeceased her husband by 24 years, dying in that very fateful year for John Burgoyne, 1776.

William Howe and the pair of junior major generals accompanying him to America on the frigate *Cerberus*, arrived at Boston in the middle of May, subsequent to the first real clash between colonists and royal troops at Lexington, Massachusetts, a month earlier, to discover that martial law and negotiation were no longer suitable tools to be employed towards conciliation; the colonies considered themselves at war.

Burgoyne also discovered that Howe's assessment of beefy, friendly, Thomas Gage, second son of Viscount Gage, originally from Sussex but who had been in America since the Braddock expedition of 1755, was correct; Gage was inept. He had once been governor of Montreal, after the defeat of France in Canada, and in 1763 became commander of all Crown forces in America, with headquarters in New York. In 1772, after a sojourn in England, Gage returned to America with four regiments to compel obedience to royal prerogatives, but after 1772 the snowballing chaos was too much for this man whose wife was the daughter of a prominent New Jersey rebel, Peter Kemble.

Thomas Gage was not disliked in the colonies until he returned to Boston with those four regiments of Crown regulars. He was a kindly, ruddy-faced, country-squire type of Englishman without much real military ability. He was relieved of his command in the autumn of 1775 and recalled to England where he was honoured, and thereafter kept out of the war.

Prior to Gage's departure, however, and subsequent to the arrival of the three major generals at Boston, colonists made noisy and derisive demonstrations, and embarrassed General Gage to the extent that he asked his new subordinate, John Burgoyne, to compose a fitting reprimand. It was done, and the first of General Burgoyne's voluminous American correspondence was worded in a manner not quite consistent with his claim that in America he would have preferred negotiating to fighting. At the same time, or a little later, General Burgoyne wrote Lord North that he was certain he could accomplish more as a Crown agent authorised to further the cause of conciliation, than as a subordinate officer in "too humble a situation to promise myself any hope of contributing essentially to His Majesty's service in the military line in America." In the same letter he also made a strong appeal to be allowed to return to England during the forthcoming winter, stating that "The private exigencies that demand my presence are very great," and it was not impossible that he was alluding to Charlotte Burgoyne's frail health.

Nothing came of Burgoyne's proposal to Lord North that he be allowed to act as an arbiter, but long before Burgoyne learned this was to be the case, he had an opportunity to observe the colonists' reaction to General Gage's sending troops to Lexington and Concord where, at the former place, they killed eight villagers and wounded ten others when armed colonists tried to bar their way. The "momentous intelligence" of this skirmish was taken throughout the colonies by post riders and word of mouth. In New York alone the colonists rioted, broke into the arsenal and seized a thousand muskets. They also commandeered a sloop laden with provisions for General Gage's troops in Boston. In Connecticut outraged volunteers were on the march within hours of getting the news. In Rhode Island armed men came from the fields and smithies, anxious to reach Boston.

Massachusetts saw hundreds of furious farmers, artisans, woodsmen hurrying towards the coast, converging at crossroads, then hastening onward again. The siege of Boston was in the making. New Hampshire raised 2000 men with no effort. Connecticut called for 6000, Massachusetts' Provincial Congress, sitting on a Sunday, called for 30,000 men eventually, and wanted 13,600 to be "immediately raised by this Province," but between mid-April when the Lexington fight took place, and June when the siege lines were fairly well established, and not counting Boston's colonial population of 20,000, of whom it was afterwards said many joined the besiegers, it was probably close to the truth to say that not less than 15,000 Americans were in place around Boston. Here, obviously, was the answer to Burgoyne's question when he, Howe and Clinton, first went ashore: How could an undisciplined rabble keep ten thousand of His Majesty's regulars cooped up in Boston?

They did it by outnumbering the regulars. The besiegers stretched in a half-circle around Boston, from the village of Roxbury to Chelsea. The centre, at Cambridge, was held by Artemus Ward with 15 Massachusetts regiments, Gridley's 4 companies of artillery, plus some volunteers from Connecticut, about 9,000 men in all. The right wing had 4,000 more men from Massachusetts, several regiments from Rhode Island, several artillery batteries, and totalled in excess of 5,000 men. The left wing, blocking access to Boston from that direction was weakest. Including New Hampshire, and more Massachusetts, volunteers, the number did not exceed 2,000 men.

This was not an army, and although Artemus Ward held nominal command on the strength of his having achieved the rank of Lieutenant Colonel during the French and Indian War, and having been appointed a Brigadier General by the Provincial Council in 1774, his health was bad, despite his early age of 48 in 1775. Fortunately for him, since logistics were shortly to cause serious trouble, the Continental Congress decided on 15th June to assume direction of the troops surrounding Boston, and appointed a Virginian, George Washington, commander. Two days after this appointment, and some time before Washington reached Boston, the battle had been fought that answered John Burgoyne's other question: Would the rabble fight?

But there was a problem facing the Americans that continually worsened as they tightened the siege lines. There was a shortage of everything; arms, ammunition, cooking utensils, blankets, food, medicine, sanitation facilities. 15,000 powerfully motivated belligerent colonists congregating in one place without direction or planning created army-size problems, and there were not very many experienced men to solve them.

The most serious shortage was in gunpowder. In April there were exactly 82 barrels. By the last week in May this had been increased to 150½ barrels. Of small arms there were plenty. Most colonists had brought along at least one musket, although some also had fowling pieces. There were few bayonets; this was to remain an almost exclusively British accoutrement for some time yet to come. There were swords and pistols, and the artillery of this 'army' consisted of several old iron cannon, a brace of howitzers, 16 pieces in all, with about six actually fit for service.

Food was almost as critical a problem as gunpowder, but some British stores were commandeered, along with a number of beeves destined for the Boston market, and with the provender either brought in by local or outlying patriots, or 'liberated' by dark night commissary patrols, the troops managed to eat fairly often.

Finally, all access and communication between Boston and the rest of Massachusetts was cut. Inside the town thousands of colonists wished to leave, and beyond, where patriot patrols posed a threat to loyalists, there were many people who wished to have the protection of Gage's regulars. A lengthy negotiation eventually resulted in an agreement to effect an exchange, but General Gage insisted that all departing colonists leave behind their armament. In this manner he was able to acquire 1778 firelock muskets, 973 bayonets, 639 pistols and 35 blunderbusses.

The condition of the blockaded British army was unenviable but far from disastrous. As long as the British owned Boston Harbour they could not be starved out, and as long as they remained alert and prepared, including the naval armament in the harbour, the Americans dared not attack the town. A stalemate, in fact, could more nearly end uncomfortably for the ill-organised colonists; at worst, for the British, it could result in a tiresome diet of salt meat and gardenpatch vegetables, plus boredom.

General Gage had made one sortie to test the landward blockade, and had seen his men pushed back into the city. After that, and for as long as the siege lasted, there were a number of little excursions and skirmishes by both sides, but no concerted effort by either to force a battle, not, that is, until five days after that proclamation John Burgoyne wrote for General Gage, denouncing the rebels, as an "infatuated multitude . . ." led by "certain well known incendiaries and traitors", who could expect "the fulness of chastisement" for their sedition. There was quite a bit more, but General Gage, deciding that proclamations were unsatisfactory, adopted an alternative course and planned to fortify Dorchester Heights on the Charles River, an eminence that overlooked Boston and which neither side up to this time sought to utilise. Gage proposed to begin the work on 18th June.

The Americans, learning of Gage's intention, on 15th June decided on a counter measure, the occupation and fortification of "Bunker's Hill", which was one of two adjoining eminences. The actual fortifications which were ultimately created were on the other, Breed's Hill (also known as Breed's pasture) which was closer to the city. Even so, the matter of which hill to fortify was debated among the Americans, many believing that because Bunker's Hill was closer to an escape route, and higher, it was preferable. In the end, pressured by impatient partisans, it was decided to erect the main fortifications on Breed's Hill and auxiliary works on Bunker's Hill. Accordingly, a redoubt eight rods square was marked out, wagons loaded with entrenching tools, hogsheads as forerunners of sandbags, gabions and fascines, were accumulated, and under cover of darkness on 16th June, about a thousand men marched forward. A detachment of Massachusetts militiamen from Colonel William

Prescott's regiment, plus 10 other volunteers were sent to Charlestown to watch for British activity. Prescott sent another company from his regiment, under Captain Hugh Maxwell, down to patrol the shore on the Boston side of the peninsula, also to watch for British movement, and finally, after wasting half the night, Colonel Prescott's men filed up the low ridge that connected Breed's Hill and Bunker Hill, the former being about 75 feet high, and the latter roughly 100 feet high.

There were only four hours of darkness left for the Americans to erect their fortifications, but they were all thoroughly accustomed to this kind of labour, being mostly farmers.

A close watch was kept on the armed vessels in the harbour, as well as on the British sentries and patrols in the city. The Americans could hear ship's bells on the half-hour, and the cry of sentries in the city reassuring one another that "All's well".

Shortly before dawn Prescott called in his patrols, and when the British awakened, and when dawnlight replaced darkness, they were astonished to discover a redoubt of formidable proportions and six feet in height overlooking their city. The captain of the *Lively*, called by the watch to see what the rebels had done during the night, put a spring on his anchor chain to bring the ship about so that her guns would bear, and opened fire. This thunderous cannonade awakened the last royalist in the city, but that is about all it really accomplished, because there was no practical way to elevate the *Lively*'s guns so that they would fire uphill.

FIVE

The Battle

It was bad enough to look out there and see that earthen redoubt without having to listen to the *Lively*'s cannonade, so orders were given for the firing to cease, but later it was resumed even though the distance was too great, the guns too light, and a proper elevation impossible to achieve. In spite of all the shelling only one American was killed, and he was outside the fortifications. Inside, two hogs-heads containing water were smashed and because it was a breathless hot day, that caused more discomfort than the hastily improvised burial ceremony.

General Gage, apprised that more rebels were strengthening the works upon the two hills, and well aware of the consequences if cannon were dragged up there overlooking his city, called a council shortly after daybreak. Clearly, the American position was poor, for aside from being surrounded on three sides by water, it was vulnerable to shelling from both the city and the bay. Reinforcements for the redoubt would have to cross the low ridge from Bunker's Hill, and that ridge was not too high for shelling by the *Lively*, the armed transport *Symmetry*, and a pair of gunboats, not to mention the *Falcon*, the *Somerset*, and the *Glasgow*, the latter very formidable with her 68 guns.

There was no doubt among the officers attending Gage's war council that the rebels had to be destroyed or driven from the heights. The issue was how this should be accomplished. Clinton allegedly favoured an immediate landing on the south side of the Neck with 500 men who would attack from the rear of the redoubt. The ships could smother the redoubt with shot so that no rebel would be able to raise up to challenge the attackers until they were atop Breed's Hill. The objective here was to separate the thirsty men in the redoubt from their allies on Bunker's Hill,

General John Burgoyne

Sir Henry Clinton

Sir Guy Carleton

William, fifth Viscount Howe

Thomas Gage

and since it was unlikely that reinforcements could survive crossing the ridge between the pair of hills, Prescott's men in the
redoubt would have to surrender.

Gage opposed this plan on the grounds that 500 men atop the
ridge behind the redoubt would be as vulnerable to the naval
shelling as they would be to rebel musket fire; also, 500 men
were unlikely to be enough once the Americans undertook to
reinforce the men in the redoubt.

An alternative plan was adopted. A strong force was to be
landed near Moulton Point on the southeast shore of the peninsula, out of range of the redoubt, and marched in a flanking
action to attack from the rear. There were not, at this time, any
breastworks that would hinder such an attack; the only fortification was Colonel Prescott's earthen redoubt.

There were, however, a number of sweating Americans working fiercely to create a breastwork. They needed, roughly, a half-
day or longer to complete their undertaking. William Howe,
writing to his brother in England, explained how the Americans
managed to have their respite. "As the shore where it was judged
most proper to land was very flat, the landing could not be made
with facility after the tide of ebb was much run off." This meant
that no landing would be undertaken until "two o'clock in the
afternoon", or well over the four to six hours the sweating dig-
gers atop their hills needed, because it was thought to be an inconvenience for the regulars to have to wade through mud to the
shore at Moulton's Point.

General Gage gave his orders: Ten companies of grenadiers,
ten of light infantry, with the 5th and 38th Regiments, were to
embark at one wharf, while the 35th grenadiers, the 43rd and
52nd infantry were to embark elsewhere. Commanding was
William Howe, a swarthy, hard-drinking, hard-living, disagreeable man, in his forty-fifth year in 1775. In reserve were the 47th,
1st Battalion of Marines, light infantry and grenadiers of the 2nd
Battalion of Marines, and of the 63rd Regiment, roughly seven
hundred men. General Howe's attack force was 1500 strong.

As soon as the embarkation was undertaken, a fierce bombardment was ordered. This was about mid-day. 28 barges conveyed
the landing party, all troops carrying full kits, blankets (it was
insufferably hot by day and only slightly cooler by night) and
cooked provisions for three days' campaigning although they

would have to climb steep hills and were never supposed to be out of sight of their support contingents.

Each foremost barge contained six brass fieldpieces to be used against rebel patrols, but when the landing was made, about one o'clock under a boiling sun, no resistance was encountered.

The troops were formed at once into three lines. General Howe strode out with a spyglass to study his objective, the earthen redoubt, and he saw that where no breastwork was supposed to be, now there was one. He also saw a great force of men over on Bunker's Hill which he assumed were reinforcements for the men in Colonel Prescott's redoubt. Obviously, his 1500 troops were not going to be adequate. Howe walked back, passed orders for the troops to break ranks, rest and eat, and sent for his reserves across the bay.

The men General Howe had thought were reinforcements were New Hampshiremen under the doughty and pragmatic John Stark, and the opinionated James Reed. When they were sent forward from Cambridge each man was issued two flints, a gill of powder, and about a pound of coarse lead (cut from the organ pipes of a Cambridge church), because there were no cartridges available. Later, during the respite Howe gave them, these men pounded their lead into slugs to fit their muskets, and had something like 15 shots to each man.

Otherwise, the British landing below Charlestown caused great confusion. Rebel troops marched in all directions, some even heading towards where the fighting would shortly erupt, but a great many went in altogether different directions, and although Artemus Ward, as commander, was kept informed, he seemed unable to perceive that Howe's landing was an attack, not a feint.

The British pushed forward two outposts: two battalions under General Howe's immediate subordinate, Brigadier General Sir Robert Pigot, at the southern base of Breed's Hill, and four companies of light infantry in a swale which protected them from enemy fire, between Howe's main force and the redoubt.

Rebels around Charlestown, which had been abandoned by most of its civilian population, harassed Pigot's troops, so, when Admiral Samuel Graves came ashore General Pigot complained to him about the "mischief his left wing sustained by the fire from Charlestown." Graves sent orders back to his squadron to use fire-shot against the town. Red-hot cannonballs were sent into Charlestown, as well as hollow cannonballs (called carcasses) filled with combustibles. Fires were started, and with no one to put them out, the entire town was shortly burning. Pigot's corps was not molested from the direction of the town after this.

Howe's reserves arrived and the entire force was drawn up into the classic battle line three ranks deep, foremost, the light infantry, then the grenadiers, and finally the 5th and 52nd Regiments, with Pigot's contingent also in place.

The artillery was sent forward to attack the three main defensive works, the redoubt, the breastworks, and a rail fence which was near the base of Bunker's Hill and which ran to the river, and which was manned, presumably, to prevent Howe from achieving a flanking position.

Howe's artillery was supported by the battery across the bay on Capp's Hill, and by Admiral Graves's ships in the bay. The cannonade was deafening, until Howe's batteries had to desist because it was found that their ammunition boxes contained 12 pound shot for 6 pound guns. Howe ordered grape shot to be used until the proper shot could be sent over, but the distance was excessive for grape, which was essentially anti-personnel ammunition, unfit for long-range bombardment. Not that this mattered greatly because the Americans crouching behind their works were badly frightened by the noise. Finally, as Howe's gunners pushed their fieldpieces forward, they got bogged down in a marsh and could not be extricated.

John Burgoyne, who had command of an artillery battery back across the bay, had an excellent view of what ensued. He shared this distinction with many others, including almost the entire population of Boston, who crowded rooftops as well as shorelines.

William Howe was too good a soldier to try a frontal attack across an open incline against fortified positions. He still thought the flanking plan feasible, and accordingly formed his troops to hit the rebel left, while making it appear he meant to strike in a frontal assault.

His front line of infantry, 11 companies, were formed on the right, towards the beach. The grenadiers, in two ranks, were in front. When the order to advance arrived, the soldiers moved ahead, still burdened with full kits, which weighed approximately one hundred pounds per man.

Howe's corps crossed the lowlands and proceeded towards the slope of Breed's Hill heading towards the rail fence and the breastwork. Pigot's corps headed toward the redoubt.

It was hard going in full pack up inclines under a blazing sun. The grass was high, making progress additionally difficult. Lines of redcoats slowed under the combined handicaps, and also to allow the artillery to go ahead and get emplaced. Every musket had a bayonet in place. Smoke from burning Charlestown mingled with smoke from the cannonade.

At the redoubt there was no sign of defenders. They were crouching below the fire-steps. Thus far in the conflict the Americans had a wholesome respect for artillery. Few of them knew anything about it, and most thought it much more formidable than it was, but nonetheless, with artillerists shelling their fortification from six different directions, the Americans had cause to worry.

In the van of the redcoat advance were the Royal Welch Fusiliers and the 23rd Regiment. Next came the 4th, or the King's Own Regiment. Orders were passed to take all objectives with the bayonet. As the advance came on, Colonel John Stark's New Hampshiremen, in three ranks behind the rail fence, held their fire until the advancing redcoats were ready to deploy to charge, a distance of about 150 feet. Then the order to fire was given. "A picture and a complication of horror and importance beyond anything that ever came to my lot to be witness to," said Burgoyne. The Royal Fusiliers were cut down by the score and the entire advance stopped still. The 4th Regiment, still advancing, pushed through the fusiliers. Another fusillade came from behind the fence. The 4th lost all its front rank and reeled back. When officers ordered the advance resumed the Americans fired another volley. The redcoat line broke and fled. The dead, it was said "lay thick as sheep in a fold".

Howe's scheme to turn the American left in order to flank the redoubt and cut it off was not going to succeed, obviously, unless he could sweep away the defenders behind the fence. The lines were re-formed, the fresh advance was begun, but at the point where the bayonet charge was to begin, the Americans, firing by ranks, dissolved the foremost redcoat line. Every man on William Howe's staff was either killed or wounded.

Finally, the British halted and returned the gunfire, which was a mistake. As stationary targets they were again decimated. When other troops came up they too were met with a withering fusillade. The entire force retreated out of range.

The Americans cheered, but their colonel, William Prescott, bald head glistening with perspiration, white cotton coat limp and filthy, went among the men warning them that they might have checked the British, but make no mistake about it, those redcoats would be back.

William Howe, black in the face, his uniform dark with sweat, reformed the ranks and within a half hour was prepared for his next assault. The light infantry was to feint towards that lethal fence to hold the defenders in place, while Howe and Robert Pigot hurled their combined force against the redoubt and the breastworks. This time there would be no halting to allow the artillery to pass through and get emplaced.

The advance was undertaken without a sound coming from the rebel works. Howe's force marched to within a hundred feet of the objectives, then deployed in line of battle and opened fire. The Americans did as they had so effectively done before. They fired in volley form with each rank reloading while the other ranks fired. Smoke enveloped not only the redoubt, but also the breastworks and the fence.

The advancing redcoats, stumbling over the dead and injured, struggled to advance, their purpose, once they had discharged their muskets, to charge with bayonets, but such a manoeuvre against the devastating fire, as one observer noted, was impossible. "Most of our Grenadiers and Light-infantry, the moment of presenting themselves, lost three-fourths, and many nine-tenths of their men. Some had only eight or nine men a company left; some only three, four and five."

A retreat was begun, hastened along by that furious fire from the defences. After the British withdrawal, although the Americans had time to be reinforced, this did not happen. But a number of the injured and dazed wandered away. Many left "—because they had been all night and day on fatigue, without sleep, victuals, or drink."

Howe now received nearly half a thousand more reinforcements, the 2nd Marines and 63rd Regiment, from his reserve, the men sent for after the first assault. He promptly began ordering

his lines for another attack, but now there was protest that to go
into that terrible fire again was plain butchery. Howe ignored
the remonstrances and ordered (finally) all unnecessary equip-
ment to be left behind, including those 100-pound kits. He
directed that the artillery be taken to a position east of the breastwork and west of the rail fence where its fire could enfilade the
breastwork's defenders. Then, he ordered the troops to advance
by columns again, without firing a shot, to storm the defences
with bayonets.

Henry Clinton, on Capp's Hill across the bay, had had enough
inactivity. He crossed to the peninsula, gathered all the wounded
and service troops available, and undertook a second advance by
columns.

The Americans had to demolish cannon shot to secure the
charge for loading their muskets. There was no reserve of
powder left, and although appeals went out, no powder or lead
arrived before the British advance was seen coming up the slopes
again.

Howe's artillery successfully enfiladed the breastwork and its
defenders were driven away. Clinton and Pigot, concentrating
on the redoubt, sent their combined force at the charge. Lord
Rawdon said, "The Americans rose up and poured in so heavy a
fire upon us that the oldest officers say they never saw a sharper
action." But this time that ". . . most sore and deadly fire" lacked
its previous sustaining power as shot pouches and powderhorns
became empty.

Redcoats poured over the defences, the noise was deafening,
and because the defenders could only use clubbed muskets against
bayonets, a British marine said, the slaughter was shocking, but
as a matter of fact, aside from powder smoke, the dust was so
thick once the fighting was confined to the redoubt that the
British, unable to tell friend from enemy, held back, and all
but about thirty or forty of Prescott's defenders managed to
escape.

Several hundred yards distant about a thousand Americans
stood on Bunker's Hill and watched. They could have struck
the British rear, but instead they did not even give fire-support
to their fleeing comrades from Breed's Hill. Even so, and John
Burgoyne noted this, the defeated defenders did not rout, but,
according to Lord Rawdon, persisted in a "running fight from

one fence or wall to another, till we entirely drove them off the peninsula."

As soon as they had withdrawn far enough to be secure, on the Cambridge Road, the Americans immediately began to erect new fortifications. As before, they worked all night and created a respectable entrenchment, but the British did not come in pursuit. They busied themselves reinforcing and garrisoning the captured fortifications on Breed's and Bunker's Hills.

William Howe's losses were sanguinary. Of approximately 2,400 men who had participated, 226 had been killed, out of 1,054 who had been shot, including 92 officers. Howe's personal staff, 12 officers, had been wiped out. There were 4 survivors of the King's Own Regiment able to stand muster. Only 3 remained of the Royal Welch Fusiliers. Brigadier General Earl Percy, son of the Duke of Northumberland, wrote his father that "My Regiment, being one of the first that entered the redoubt, is almost entirely cut to pieces; there are but 9 men left in my company and not above 5 in one of the others."

John Burgoyne, in a letter to Lord Rochfort, Secretary of State for the Colonies, at the same time that he said Thomas Gage should have been more energetic in his earlier response to the rebel's defiance, also noted that "The principle of seizing arms, and thereby bringing the designs of the malcontents to a test and a decision was certainly just."

He also noted in this letter that "my friend Howe's conduct will not want my testimony to do it justice. Clinton had the good fortune in the course of the action to be actively employed, and acquitted himself well. . . . For my part, the inferiority of my station as youngest Major-General upon the staff, left me almost a useless spectator, for my whole business lay in presiding during part of the action over a cannonade to assist the left." Concerning the enemy, whom he had previously held in contempt, Burgoyne wrote that "The defence was well conceived and obstinately maintained; the retreat was no flight; it was even covered with bravery and military skill, and proceeded no farther than to the next hill, where a new post was taken, new entrenchments instantly begun."

With respect of the disproportionate number of casualties among British officers Burgoyne said ". . . there is a melancholy reason for it. Let it not pass even in a whisper from your

Lordship to more than one person [the King?]: The zeal and intrepidity of the officers, which was without exception exemplary, was ill seconded by the private men. Discipline, not to say courage, was wanting. In the critical moment of carrying the redoubt, the officers of some corps were almost alone; and what was the worst part of the confusion of these corps – all the wounds of the officers were not received from the enemy."

This last allegation was correct, but as time passed it was found not to be exclusive to the British. The uniform of the rebel General David Wooster was preserved for many years, showing a bullet hole in the back.

If Burgoyne had found an answer to his earlier question concerning the courage of the colonists, so had General Gage, who wrote Lord Dartmouth, the enemy was not "the despicable rabble too many have supposed them to be."

There had been other meetings between Crown troops and Americans – Lexington, Concord. Ticonderoga – but nothing equal to the peninsular battle known as Bunker's Hill, or the Siege of Boston, of which it was the termination. Out of this engagement came a frank and necessary assessment and comparison of the opponents, not only the officers and men, but also the purposes, motivations, and objectives, because clearly enough this was to be a prolonged and desperate struggle, the kind where all aspects required scrutiny and study.

As John Burgoyne said, "Driven from one hill, you will see the enemy continually retrenched upon the next; and every step we move must be the slow step of siege."

SIX

Aftermath

"We certainly are victorious," wrote a Londoner when news of the Battle of Bunker's Hill reached Europe, "but if we have eight more such victories there will be nobody left to bring the news of them." In the House of Commons, John Wilkes said, "What have we conquered? Bunker's Hill with the loss of 1,200 men. Are we to pay as dearly for the rest of America?" Colonel Barré, who had opposed the Stamp Act, thought the action at Bunker's Hill "smacked more of defeat than victory," Thomas Gage received the blame, when blame was forthcoming, and when praise was offered it went to William Howe. Although there was a good deal of recrimination over the losses, King George was satisfied with "the firmness of spirit which distinguished the troops. . . ."

Lord North was not quite as unfeeling, although he remained His Majesty's pawn when he wrote Burgoyne that "The gallantry and ability of General Howe, and the bravery of the men he commanded on 17th June, are the admiration of their countrymen, but the number of wounded and killed makes my heart bleed. I would abandon the contest were I not most intimately convinced in my own conscience that our cause is just and important."

John Burgoyne described the action differently to different people. In a letter to his brother-in-law, Lord Stanley, he wrote:

To consider this action as a soldier, it comprised . . . almost every branch of military duty and curiosity. Troops landed in the face of an enemy; a fine disposition; a march sustained by a powerful cannonade . . . a deployment from the march to form for the attack of the entrenchments and redoubt; a vigorous defence; a storm with bayonets; a large and fine town set on fire by shells. Whole streets of houses, ships upon the stocks, a number of churches, all sending up volumes of smoke and flame, or falling together in ruin, were capital objects . . . the steeples of Boston, and the masts of such ships as were unemployed in the harbour, all crowded with spectators, friends and foes, alike in anxious suspense, made a back-ground to the piece, and the whole together composed a representation of war that I think the imagination of Le Brun never reached. It was great, it was high spirited, and while the animated impression remains, let us quit it.

It was as well to "quit it" after that stirring description for otherwise Burgoyne would have had to mention the aftermath, seen through other eyes in this way:

It is impossible to describe the horror that on every side presented itself (in Boston) — wounded and dead officers in every street; the town, which is larger than New York, almost uninhabited . . . bells tolling, wounded soldiers lying in their tents and crying for assistance to remove some men who had just expired. So little precaution did General Gage take to provide for the wounded by making hospitals, that they remained in this deplorable situation for three days.

In Britain a gentleman named Wedderburn wrote Lord North that "This country is never sufficiently prepared. The misconduct of the General (Gage) and the Admiral (Graves) is the most obvious cause of the present bad posture of affairs in America." Wedderburn's further indignation led him to suggest that Gage and Graves be recalled. Both were. Vice Admiral Samuel Graves appointed in March 1777 to command British naval forces in America was overwhelmingly master of the North American waterways with no less than 25 war vessels, yet he appeared fearful of the rebel fleets of whale boats and did very little to oppose them. In August 1775 Burgoyne asked Lord George Germain, Secretary of State for the American Colonies and also for the American War, what "is the Admiral doing?" And the answer could have been — nothing. Graves was re-called in December.

Thomas Gage, fairly well vilified in letters going from Boston to London by almost everyone who wrote of conditions in the colonies, where Gage was commander, including Burgoyne, was eventually given the King's order recalling him on 2nd August. Major General William Howe was given command of the army, and at once he ordered the evacuation of Boston.

Although militarily justified, the order was met with great out-
cries not only from the military who viewed it as a loss of face,
but from the unfortunate Tories whose homes and shops there
would have to be abandoned.

New York was thought to be a more signal and central location for British headquarters in North America. Certainly, it was
more distant from what appeared to be the hub and heart of rebel
opposition, for subsequent to the Bunker Hill engagement, and
with General Washington commanding, the Americans were not
only besieging Boston again, but they created a force of small,
swift ships with which they harassed British shipping, and
because everything used to supply the British came into Boston
harbour by ship, this was an insufferable annoyance. It also posed
some critical problems, as when ships bringing coal were captured by Americans, and during the bitter New England winter
His Majesty's troops had to demolish a number of churches,
wharves, residences, ships, and fences as well as trees, to keep
warm. One elm yielded 14 cords of wood. It must have been an
enormous tree.

Smallpox raged in epidemic proportions, the ill and wounded
suffered from a want of fresh fruit and vegetables, and aside from
a general demoralisation, there was the appalling boredom.

Burgoyne and Henry Clinton agreed with William Howe,
and even Thomas Gage concurred, that "no offensive operations
can be carried on to advantage from Boston." But there was one
excellent reason why the British could not move to New York
that autumn or winter; they did not have sufficient transports.

About this time Burgoyne became involved in a unique correspondence. On 7th June, even before the battle, a letter was
addressed to him from Charles Lee, now a US Major General.
"My Dear Sir," wrote Lee, "it is a duty I owe to the friendship I
have long and sincerely professed for you; a friendship to which
you have the strongest claims from the first moment of our
acquaintance . . . that makes me . . . entreat and conjure you . . .
to impute these lines not to a petulant itch of scribbling, but to
the most unfeigned solicitude for the future tranquility of your
mind, and for your reputation. I sincerely lament the infatuation
of the times, when men of such a stamp as Mr Burgoyne and Mr
Howe can be seduced into so impious and nefarious a service, by
the artifice of a wicked and insidious court and cabinet."

There was a good deal more, all of it denouncing the King, the government's suppression of liberty at home as well as in the colonies, and all of it reflecting the cynical bitterness of a man whose valour no one ever doubted, but whose judgment, and subsequently whose obedience – he was court-martialled by the Americans in 1778 – could very easily be questioned. Nevertheless Burgoyne answered on 8th July, saying, among other things, that "When we were last together in service, (in Portugal) I should not have thought it within the vicissitude of human affairs that we should meet at any time, or in any sense, as foes." Then he suggests a personal meeting. "Above all, I should find an interview happy if it should induce such explanations as might tend in their consequence to peace."

Both Lee's and Burgoyne's letters were seen and studied on both sides, and it is entirely possible that Burgoyne's proposal of a meeting was managed with William Howe's approval, and with a view towards offering amnesty and money to Charles Lee (subsequently done with Benedict Arnold) in order that the British might acquire a high-ranking American officer as their ally.

But no meeting ever took place. When Lee asked for approval of the meeting in a letter to the Provincial Congress of Massachusetts, he received the following reply:

Watertown, July 10, 1775.

Sir:

The Congress have perused the letter from Genl. Burgoyne, which you was kind enough to submit to their inspection. They can have no objection to the proposed interview, from a want of the highest confidence in the wisdom, discretion, and integrity of Genl Lee, but beg leave to suggest that as the confidence of the people in their General is so essentially necessary to the well-conducting of the enterprise in which we are engaged, and as a people contending for their liberties are actually disposed to jealousy, and not inclined to make the most favourable construction of the motives of conduct which they are not fully acquainted with, whether such an interview might not have a tendency to lessen the influence which the Congress would wish to extend to the utmost of their power to facilitate and succeed the operations of war. . . ."

The following day Charles Lee wrote Burgoyne from Cambridge, that although he "Would be extremely happy in the interview he [Burgoyne] so kindly proposed", knowing that

General Burgoyne had already made up his mind it was impossible that General Lee should alter his opinion. Lee closed by saying that Burgoyne's cause must fail because "he knows Great Britain cannot stand the contest."

This concluded the correspondence, except that Burgoyne, in some of his letters to England's leaders and others at home, gave his opinion of how such a meeting would have proceeded, and along with those observations, also, as usual, offered advice about how the American campaign should be prosecuted. Simultaneously, he again brought up the matter of his returning to England, and during this period – August 1775 – he was drafted to answer a letter of complaint from the American Commander-in-Chief, George Washington.

There was bitterness among the Americans that some of their captured officers in Boston had been lodged in a jail and otherwise mistreated. Washington made a good point by saying:

Let your opinion, Sir, of the principle which actuates [the prisoners] be what it may, they suppose they act from the noblest of all principles, a love of freedom and their country. But political opinions . . . are foreign to this point; the obligations arising from the rights of humanity and claims of rank, are universally binding and extensive. . . . These I should have hoped would have dictated a more tender treatment of those individuals whom chances of war has put in your power.

Burgoyne's answer, signed by Gage, to whom Washington's letter had been addressed, was understandably pithy.

To the glory of civilised nations, humanity and war have been made compatible, and compassion to the subdued is almost a general system.

Britons, ever pre-eminent in mercy, have outgone common examples, and overlooked the criminal in the captive.

Upon these principles your prisoners . . . have hitherto been treated with care and kindness – indiscriminately, it is true, for I acknowledge no rank that is not derived from the king. My intelligence from your army would justify severe recrimination. I understand there are some of the King's faithful subjects, taken from time to time by the rebels, now labouring like negro slaves to gain their daily subsistence; while others are reduced to the wretched alternative to perish by famine or take up arms against their King and country . . .

In Boston during the late summer and autumn of 1775 there was little else for John Burgoyne to do except write. Aside from attending to a heavy correspondence with the influential men he had been exchanging letters with since arriving in America, Burgoyne wrote a play. *The Blockade of Boston*, in August, and the following month wrote the prologue for a play entitled *Zara*. There was little other than improvised amusement to occupy the British in Boston while they awaited sufficient shipping to abandon the place. But there actually was very little hardship. Supplies arriving from England — although only a fraction actually reached America — and Nova Scotia, as well as those sent from the West Indies, prevented hunger, which was perhaps the most critical possibility, but otherwise the British were under a more efficient siege than before. The Americans were not only strongly entrenched and well supplied, but they numbered 17,000 men, and with ample time for it, they were learning something about military discipline and close-order drill. There was one very serious flaw in all this: by the last day of December every enlistment would expire. Washington and many others, in Congress and elsewhere, feared the consequences if the men did not re-enlist. There was good reason to believe that many men would not, would pack up and return home. A siege was not the best way to sustain high morale, inside Boston or outside of it.

But for the British in Boston during August and September, Washington's dilemma of three months hence was not a very relevant factor. Burgoyne, in a particularly lengthy letter on 20th August, concluded with a fresh allusion to his desire to return home with the coming of winter, when there would not be much possibility for military activity. He said that he had "hopes that a scheme which I have proposed to combine with my return may be of assistance to the great general cause. The present occasion does not permit me to open myself farther upon that head."

He had a "scheme", and without being aware of it, the King had hoped he might. Much earlier His Majesty had told Lord North that Burgoyne should be allowed to return ". . . as it will be of importance to his private affairs, and he will besides be able to bring a very full account of the minds and dispositions of the people of that part of the globe . . ."

Thomas Gage sailed for England in October, when William

Howe assumed full command. General Burgoyne prepared to sail from Boston two months later, and on the 1st December Charles Lee wrote him another letter, this one exhorting Burgoyne to immortalise himself as "the saviour of your country." According to Lee "The whole British Empire stands tottering on the brink of ruin", and Burgoyne had it in his power "to prevent the fatal catastrophe."

The letter was more like a religious tract than a communication from one soldier to another, except that there was a subtle implication that, precisely as Burgoyne appears to have entertained an idea of subverting Lee, so did Lee also have some idea that he might do the same for Burgoyne.

Nothing came of this correspondence. In fact Burgoyne and Charles Lee never wrote one another again. They never met again either, although it would have been impossible for each not to have heard of the events that crowded into one another's lives until Lee died in 1782, with the fact that he had actually and secretly betrayed the Americans while a British prisoner, generally unknown.

When Burgoyne finally boarded the *Boyne*, the chill of a New England winter lay everywhere in his sight, and he cannot have felt anything but tremendous relief to be quitting so untidy, smelly, confining, and demoralising a place as Boston.

SEVEN

A Variation of Enemies

By the time John Burgoyne sailed for England in December of 1775, not only the British in Boston had met the enemy. The small garrison at Fort Ticonderoga surrendered to a rebel force under Ethan Allen of Vermont and Benedict Arnold of Connecticut. The old fort, strategically located at a narrow place where Lake George emptied into Lake Champlain, on an eminence a hundred feet high on the western escarpment, was considered a "key to the gateway to the continent" providing invaders came southward into New England from Canada, or went northward from New England. In 1775 it was considered a valuable outpost by the Americans because Governor Carleton in loyal Canada might eventually pose a threat. The fear in some American quarters was that sooner or later the royalists would use Canada as a staging area, build up a strong force, then march southward and split the colonies apart so that first one dismembered segment could be conquered, then the other segment could be conquered. It was not a fresh idea; the French, when they had been masters of Canada, had considered it.

Elsewhere, in Virginia, the royal governor, Lord Dunmore, had been compelled to flee for his life, and in New York, Tories were driven from their homes. Yet there was a great division of opinion, so that when the royal governor, William Tryon, returned to New York from a visit to England, he was given a cordial welcome – on the same day that many of the same New Yorkers welcomed several American field commanders.

The American commander Richard Montgomery, took Montreal in November 1775, then co-operated with Benedict Arnold in an attack upon Quebec on the last day of December 1775. The attack failed, Richard Montgomery was killed, and Arnold's sad

General Horatio Gates

Benedict Arnold

Bunker's Hill, or the Blessed Effects of Family Quarrels
America (a Red Indian woman) wrestles with Britannia. Spain
(left) and France encourage the dispute. Watching from a seat
on a cloud is Bute (in Scots cap and tartan waistcoat) with
his left arm around North's shoulder. A demon clutches at
Manfield on his right. One of the many satires ascribing
the American dispute to the influence of Bute

retreat ended at Crown Point, but this, called the "Kennebec Expedition," demonstrated the willingness of the colonists to carry their war to the King's soldiers.

Not long after the Kennebec Expedition foundered, far south in the Carolinas, an American force met Loyalists in a pitched battle and defeated them. Also, a seaborne British invasion, with Wilmington, Delaware and Charleston, South Carolina as objectives, met such stiff resistance that the undertaking was abandoned.

As the first year of the war ended not only had royal authority been thoroughly defied in many places, but also, British arms had been successfully resisted. Yet, in part because the American invasion of Canada was a failure, and regardless of the fact that Howe was besieged in Boston and the British had not been able to secure a fresh foothold anywhere in the colonies, 1775 actually ended in a stalemate.

American morale was high, which was what made it possible for Washington to create a new army out of the vast armed rabble he had inherited around Boston as the winter of 1775 closed in. It also helped the rebel cause that some months would pass before reinforcements for the British arrived. During this period of relative inactivity on the various fighting fronts more and more Americans veered towards the radical viewpoint of total independence. There was no longer any trade with Great Britain, and His Majesty had rejected the American petition for the redress of grievances, and with the consent of Parliament had hired German troops – "Hessians" – to fight in America. It was also said the British would employ Indians, would pay a bounty for colonial scalps.

What had been a civil war became a rebellion. As time passed orators like Adams, Jefferson, Henry, called for a revolution against tyranny, and writers like Tom Paine, in his *Common Sense*, made converts by the thousands. The prevailing opinion came to favour a complete overthrow of imperial rule.

Those who had held out for, if not a reconciliation, then at least some form of commonwealth association, were alienated by the King's hiring of mercenaries. They viewed the use of Germans, Brunswickers and Hessians as only slightly better than the use of Indians. Of the latter the colonists with good cause had a very low opinion. Before the war had been renewed for very long, in 1776, the British, too, would regret their employment of Indians.

Otherwise, the two forces that were to contend so fiercely between the first major battle – Bunker Hill in 1775 – and the last battle – Yorktown in 1781 – were not very similar at the fighting level, which would be where the battles would be won and lost. The Americans, never having had an army, called their troops militia, meaning that every able-bodied man of a province between the ages of 16 and 60 was required by law to belong to the armed company of his township. Subsequent to the French and Indian War of 1754, which was the North American extension of the Seven Years War, several volunteer regiments were raised in the colonies, with officers appointed as political expediency required. But eventually these units were disbanded and the Americans returned to the village militia system, with the difference that many militiamen having gained experience as sometime soldiers in the regiments, helped make some militia units passable soldiering contingents.

When war with Britain was imminent, and because many militia officers were Loyalists, it was proposed that every village supplying men to the rebellion elect local officers, whose sympathies were with the rebellion, and who would choose the field commanders. These men, one-third of whom were to be ready to muster "at a minute's notice", hence the name "Minutemen", were not uniformed. They paraded, drilled, and eventually marched to war in every variety of attire from buckle shoes to moccasins, from frock coats to leather shirts.

Their armament, particularly in New England where the war began, was equally varied. At this time, in 1775, the rifled gun was almost unheard of in New England. It came into the war later, from the western areas of Pennsylvania, and the southern provinces of Virginia and Maryland, where, according to John Adams, these unique weapons were in the hands of "the most accurate marksmen in the world."

Otherwise the Americans were armed with blunderbusses, fowling pieces, Brown Bess muskets from the French and Indian War, and guns from much earlier conflicts, King George's War and Queen Anne's War. There were also a number of homemade muskets, some firing thumb-size leaden projectiles. Every village had its gunsmith.

Accompanying this assortment of weapons were knives, pistols, axes, tomahawks, and pikes, which were 12 feet long with pointed iron spearheads, not to mention home-made swords of great weight and thickness. There were powderhorns, bullet moulds and shot pouches, along with extra bags of flints, and while British regulars were given a standard allotment of 60 shot, the Americans, who were always short of gunpowder, rarely came equipped with more than from 9 to 15 shot.

Very few Americans possessed bayonets, and those who had them usually had no way of affixing them to their muskets, so they wore them as swords, and also found them very useful for spits while cooking. The bayonet would remain an almost exclusively British weapon until such European drillmasters as Baron von Steuben taught the Americans how to use it, as late as 1777.

Benjamin Franklin suggested overcoming the gunpowder shortage through the use of bows and arrows, but this idea was not very favourably received for a number of reasons.

The rifle, when it was brought to the conflict, proved to be a mixed blessing. Response to Congress's edict that "six companies of expert riflemen, be immediately raised in Pennsylvania, two in Maryland and two in Virginia, "each to be composed of 68 privates and their elected officers, caused an unprecedented response. In Pennsylvania the companies were so over-subscribed that an entire battalion was mustered under Colonel William Thompson. Virginia's riflemen, buckskin and moccasin clad, included the renowned warrior, Daniel Morgan, and among Maryland's rifleman was the famous Indian fighter, Michael Cresap.

Predominantly, these men, mostly tall and rugged, were of Scotch-Irish descent. They had been hunting and fighting since boyhood, and while their valour, like their marksmanship, was above question, their independence of spirit and quick tempers made them very difficult to discipline. At the siege of Boston, following the Bunker Hill battle, these restless, active individualists broke the monotony by creeping close to the town, and at ranges no musket was even remotely accurate at, picked off British sentries. Washington's friend, Joseph Reed, said that the riflemen were ". . . grown so terrible to the [British] regulars, that nothing is to be seen over the breastwork but a hat."

General Washington, unlike many of the enlisted men, took no delight in this sniping on the grounds that it was a waste of ammunition, and because he was never sure the riflemen would not precipitate a battle. Remonstrances did no good, and when the riflemen had succeeded in causing more than a little turmoil, General Washington said "he wished they had never come". General Charles Lee ". . . damned them and wished them all in Boston", and another American officer said they were as "Indifferent men as I ever served with . . . mutinous . . . unwilling for Duty of any kind . . . and I think the army . . . would be as well without them as with them."

The trouble was simply that these were not men accustomed to prolonged inactivity. They had come to fight and that was what they wished to do. Later, in action, many an American commander was proud of them, and many a Royal Commander, including John Burgoyne, would have reason to deplore them.

British enlisted men called the rifled gun of these men a "Widow and orphan maker." It was not native to the colonies, having been developed in Europe, but the American variation, the so-called Kentucky rifle, actually the Pennsylvania rifle, much lighter, more graceful, and longer than the European rifled weapon, was exclusively American.

Sometimes the Kentucky rifle was as much as 5 feet in length. It was usually expertly hand-crafted, quite light in an age when military muskets were very heavy, and fired a ball weighing half an ounce. Riflemen astonished friend and foe alike by hitting a patch 7 inches in diameter at 250 yards. Military muskets and hunting weapons of the time were totally inaccurate under most conditions and did not fire a ball more than 125 yards.

But the musket could be loaded faster. Also, because the musket threw a solid lead slug, at close quarters it was better. The half-ounce rifle bullet did not always put a man down. Very seldom did an enemy hit by a lead slug fired at close range from a smooth-bore musket get to his feet again.

In order for the rifle ball to have contact with the rifling in a barrel, a small patch of cloth or buckskin was placed atop the barrel's muzzle, the ball was laid on the patch, and both were then rammed home to make a snug fit for the ball, which, when the rifle was fired, gained its remarkable momentum from the twisting grooves in the rifled barrel. A musket, because it required no patch and less care, could be loaded and fired in half the time. But, whatever the rifle's drawbacks, it was the best long-range weapon in the hands of enlisted men throughout the entire war, far superior to the British or American muskets.

As for the men who handled both, on the American side, they were never entirely amenable to discipline, nor were they always predictable on the field, but after 1775 they shared an increasingly common zeal, an idea of American independence. Also, and perhaps equally significant — possibly even more significant — the Americans were fighting on their own soil.

The British, on the other hand, were a very long way from home, in a part of the world different from their villages and shires, surrounded by a great horde of very hostile natives, and the idea prevalent at home that they would campaign in pleasant New England, through colonies full of repentant provincials, was about as erroneous as any idea could have been.

With very few exceptions everything the British soldiers used had to come by slow ship from Britain, which was not only ruinously expensive, but was also very inefficient. Hundreds of beeves died *en route*, thousands of barrels of flour spoiled, medicines, ammunition, shoes, new weapons, fell into the hands of American privateers.

There was no danger of starvation, but neither was there much opportunity to create a comfortable surplus, and therefore the spectre of dire want lingered. Gage, and after him William Howe, had plenty to worry about by the end of the year 1775.

As for their troops, in the eighteenth century the nature of Britain's army was the result of a medieval system by which the crown contracted with noblemen and others to raise regiments, much as John Burgoyne had raised his 16th Light Dragoons. The government paid a commanding officer for each enlistee, and subsequently an annual amount for his care. Commanders sold commissions in their regiments and these subordinates could in turn re-sell their commissions, and purchase higher ones. Most commonly, this was how subordinates became superiors, by buying a higher rank. If an officer lacked the money to 'buy up' he had to wait, usually until older officers died, then hope for advancement according to seniority.

Britain's enlisted soldier was recruited by either voluntary or compulsory methods. His pay was about 4s 6d a week. From this

he was expected to pay for medicines, clothing, and miscellan-
eous necessities. He was rarely fed adequately because officers
frequently chose to try and make money out of the annual allot-
ments, and there was no fraternising and little sympathy between
officers and men, as a general rule. The hardships enlisted men
had to endure were often as severe as those the Germans were
accustomed to. The term "bloody back" did not derive from a
regular's scarlet coat, but from the terrible lashings inflicted for
the slightest breach of discipline. One thousand lashes was a
common punishment. Soldiers were literally lashed to death.

Officers, and even English civilians, treated the common
enlisted redcoat as though he were no better than a felon. In some
instances he was no better. Because of the brutality, the poor
care, the unending hardship, voluntary enlistments in the
British army mounted to the trickle provided by "silly boys
befooled by the glamour of the scarlet coat or to men and boys
who were either desperate or drunk."

"The King's shilling"was also offered toconvicted criminals, the
choice being prison or the army. Debtors, the most commonly
imprisoned men, frequently chose oversea service to incarcera-
tion.

The "Act against vagabonds" legalised compulsory enlistment.
"Any sturdy begger, any fortune teller, any idle, unknown or
suspected fellow . . . that cannot give an account of himself . . ."
and many who could give an accounting but could be either got
drunk by the recruiter, or pummelled into abject fear, had a shilling forced into their hand.

Anyone known "as an incorrigible rogue" did not necessarily
have to be one; he only had to be so classified by the recruiter in
charge of the press gang.

Even so, and with all the zeal recruiters demonstrated, and for
which they were paid, throughout the American War, but more
particularly near the conclusion of it, the army could never
maintain its standard of strength. It was not only that the war was
an unpopular affair, the army was even more unpopular. True,
there were some enlightened commanders like John Burgoyne,
but they were too few to affect any appreciable change in the
system.

What amazed the Americans during their rebellion, and ever

after, was that all those fools and felons in scarlet coats fought so
well and died so heroically, seeming to bear out the contention
that desperate men make the best soldiers. But that would be to
ignore the matter of discipline, in which the Americans were
woefully deficient and in which the British excelled. It was this
advantage that proved time and again that whatever the back-
ground of King George's troops at home, in North America they
usually behaved better in camp and on the march than did their
foemen.

In battle, it was that steady advance by columns, the product of
perfect discipline, that routed so many Americans. That, and the
British artillery, were most feared. Eventually, the Americans
became accustomed to the cannons, which were not very accurate, but they never quite got accustomed to those scarlet ranks
advancing, bayonets extended, loaded muskets at the ready, perfectly disciplined.

British regiments were composed of eight companies of ordin-
ary infantry, one company of light infantry, and one company of
grenadiers. The light infantry was for reconnaissance, outpost,
and skirmish duty. The grenadiers, all tall men, although originally recruited and trained for the purpose of hurling small iron
hand-bombs in 1678, were armed like the rest of the infantry by
the time they arrived in America. The little iron hand-bomb, or
grenade, had become obsolete. British commanders were convinced it had no future. These grenadiers retained their tall,
brimless helmets, whose mitre-like appearance was to become so
popular with American illustrators after the war that one might
almost have believed the entire British army was composed of
grenadiers.

The strength of a British regiment was supposedly 477 men,
but throughout the rebellion shortages predominated. For example, in early 1775, General Gage's regiments actually numbered
closer to 292 men, rank and file. By June, when he got a contingent of light horse, the 17th dragoons, he could boast of one
nearly full-strength unit. The 17th Light Dragoons numbered
400 men. Like all light horse outfits, they were armed with a
musket, or carbine, a brace of pistols, and a sword, and although
they rode to battle, unlike the cavalry which fought from the
saddle, light dragoons dismounted and entered combat on foot.

In another way the British differed greatly from the Americans

– in uniforms. Very few American companies had uniforms until the second and third years of the war, but the British arrived in America in attire copied from the resplendent German infantry.

This included the scarlet coat, decorated with lace, brass buttons, facings, and ·coloured lining. The standing collars were reinforced to a stiffness that impeded head movement, which was additionally hampered by the regulation high stock under the jaw. The sleeves were tight, hindering ready arm movement.

Beneath the coat was worn a waistcoat, scarlet or white, and tightly buttoned. The breeches, also white, were tight, as were the buttoned gaiters that came above the knee.

The belt, to be worn snug, held the bayonet scabbard. A strap from the left shoulder crossing the chest held the cartridge box on the right hip. Hats ranged from the most common triangular felt type, to the visorless grenadier helmets, to bearskin shakos, neither of which offered any protection at all to the eyes when marching under a blinding sun.

The hair was usually clubbed at the back and held in place with grease and white powder. The same grease and powder treatment was applied to the artificial curls worn in front of the ears up each side of the head. Braiding and dressing the hair was a lengthy procedure. In fact, for the average British enlisted man to prepare himself for parade or combat required about two hours, and he had to have help putting his queue in shape.

The common weapon of the infantryman was his Brown Bess musket, whose name derived from Queen Elizabeth 1, under whose aegis the first matchlocks were introduced into the army, and also from the fact that the metal parts including the muzzle, had been browned. The Brown Bess was a smooth-bore weapon, weighed approximately 10 pounds, was 54 inches tall, and was fitted to accommodate the regulation 21-inch British bayonet. It fired a ball weighing more than an ounce, and because it was almost invariably over-charged, and recoiled very painfully when fired, was quite commonly held too high for accuracy. This was difficult to attain in any case, less because the weapon was not true, than because the average British enlisted man was not a good shot. The reason he was not lay in the fact that he was never taught to take aim at a specific enemy. As G. M. Trevelyan noted, he "was taught to point his weapon horizontally, brace himself for a vicious recoil and pull a ten-pound trigger till his gun went off: if, indeed, it did go off when the hammer fell."

Loading this weapon involved biting off the end of a cylinder containing powder and ball, shaking some powder into the pan, dropping the butt of the musket to the ground smartly, pouring more powder into the barrel, shaking some of the powder into the touchhole, ramming home the ball and patch, then raising the musket to fire.

When the trigger was pulled and the hammer fell, striking its flint against a bit of steel the *frizzen* (sparks) fell on the powder in the pan – and hopefully – ignited it. There were then two sputtering spurts of flame, one towards the touchhole, the other inward to the charge, and after a decent interval of agonised waiting, for the soldier, there was a smoky, loud explosion, and the slug was projected.

Actually, the Brown Bess musket was most serviceable as the handle from which to suspend that long, gleaming, regulation bayonet, and it can be deduced by the preference given this weapon by British field commanders, that they did not hold the Brown Bess musket in very high regard. It was customary to do as General Howe's troops had done at Bunker's Hill: Advance the redcoat line to within less than a hundred yards of the enemy, then to fire one ineffectual volley and charge with the bayonet. These attacks were usually successful. They were also the most unnerving assault the Americans had to face, and throughout the war rebel troops broke and fled before them, unless supported by ranks of riflemen trained to stand and fire, as happened twice at the engagement on 17th June 1775.

These, then, were the men, weapons, and organisations opposing one another at the outbreak of initial hostilities and up until General Burgoyne sailed home in December 1775 to acquaint His Majesty's councils with what England had to contend with in the New World. Neither side would change very much in the bloody years ahead, or until about 1779 when the Americans, finally uniformed and outfitted as soldiers, trained by competent Europeans, and with foreign allies, French and Spanish, were able to wear down their enemy.

EIGHT

Moves and Countermoves

In England it was generally known that the Americans under Montgomery had taken Montreal, and that more Americans under Ethan Allen and Benedict Arnold had marched through the Maine wilderness towards Quebec. By the time John Burgoyne arrived home it was erroneously assumed that Canada had fallen to the rebels.

No one entertained much hope that the inhabitants of French-speaking Canada would help the British. In fact many Britons, recalling Wolfe's opinion of these people (he called them "vermin") were not sure that their help, if it were offered, should be accepted. To many an Englishman the whole of North America was a quicksand of deceit and treachery, regardless of whether, New England or the former French provinces, came under discussion.

The Cabinet had not been unanimous in its feelings when it had looked as though the mother country was an overpowering bully. After a fresh look in late 1775 it decided that everything should be done that could be done towards re-establishing the royal authority in America, and towards preventing Britain's troops from being evicted.

If, as it seemed, New England might be lost, concerted steps should be taken that a similar fate did not befall Canada, for which James Wolfe, among others, had paid with his life.

General Burgoyne had written before leaving America that he had a plan in mind upon which he preferred at that time not to elaborate. He could explain now, when he was invited to the war councils in England, that his plan involved a fresh military concept by which Canada would be made safe, and at the same time a means for a vigorous, fresh thrust south-ward into New England could be implemented.

This hypothesis was outlined in a well-written treatise entitled "Reflections upon the War in America", in which Burgoyne shared the prevalent view that Quebec had been taken. Other-wise his plan was appropriate to actual existing conditions.

It appeared to Burgoyne that two armies, one from the north in Canada and one from the south, should march to a juncture cutting the colonies into two separate sectors, after which the separated areas could be conquered individually. The coastal seg-ment should additionally be blockaded by "a number of . . . armed vessels, from the sloop of eighty or ninety tons to the row-boat. Each of the great ships, frigates and sloops of war, would thus resemble a primary planet with its satellites oscillating round it. . . ."

Burgoyne sensibly thought the troops should be outfitted for the kind of war they were engaged in, instead of as European troops on parade. Also, although he had little sympathy for the American cause, and even less sympathy for some individual Americans, in total he gave them a grudging respect.

> They are ever ready at earthworks and palisading, [he wrote,] and they will cover and entrench themselves wherever they are for a short time left unmolested with surprising alacrity. . . it may be said . . . that every private man will in action be his own general, who will turn every tree and bush into a kind of temporary fortress, from whence, when he hath fired his shot with all the deliberation, cool-ness, and certainty which hidden safety inspires, he will skip as it were to the next, and so on for a long time till dislodged either by cannon or by a resolute attack of light infantry. In this view of the American militia, rebels as they are, they will be found to be respect-able even in flight. Light infantry, therefore, in greater numbers than one company per regiment, ought to be an essential part of the general system of our army."

But he also made a pardonable mistake. "It is not to be expected," he wrote, "that the rebel Americans will risk a gen-eral combat or a pitched battle, or even stand at all, except behind entrenchments as at Boston."

Prior to the Bunker's Hill fight the "rebel Americans" had not stood very well, but in those preliminary skirmishes they had not been at all sure they wanted to stand and fight After Lexington,

Concord, and Bunker's Hill, they were convinced that fighting was the only recourse left them.

In stressing the value of dividing the colonies by marching two separate armies to a juncture, Burgoyne did not think the southern force should come north from New York because of transportation and supply difficulties.

The plan that was finally adopted advocated that the fleet under Admiral Lord Howe should cooperate closely with the army under the admiral's brother, General William Howe, in taking and holding New York, while farther southward, a strong force under General Henry Clinton and Sir Peter Parker should reduce the southern colonies. At the same time Sir Guy Carleton, Governor of Canada — later Baron Dorchester — should employ his Canadian forces in expelling the Americans from his province.

It was a good plan. It implied vigour and an unrelenting attitude towards the King's enemies in North America, but if John Burgoyne expected an individual command, which seems quite likely, he had to be content with less. In February 1776 he was appointed Second in Command of Canadian forces under Sir Guy Carleton, "a distant, reserved" man, noted for "a rigid strictness in his manner which is very unpleasing and which he observes even to his most particular friends and acquaintances."

Guy Carleton was not likeable, but of all the British commanders in America he was the coolest and most capable. That His Majesty would ultimately think otherwise changed nothing.

Before the strategy of divide and conquer could be fairly implemented General Washington convinced General Howe that the time had come for a British evacuation of Boston. Washington sent a youthful colonel of artillery, Henry Knox, the 250-pound son of a shipmaster, to Fort Ticonderoga to remove the guns and bring them to Washington at Boston. It was a feat of incredible hardship and at one time the largest iron cannon broke through the ice and sank into the Hudson. Knox fished it up and pressed onward. He crossed and re-crossed the river four times and employed 80 yoke of oxen, eventually arriving at Washington's encampment with an impressive train of heavy guns including 8 brass and 6 iron mortars, a howitzer, as well as 30 iron and 13 brass guns. One cannon was a 24-pounder. The others ranged from 12- to 18-pounders. Some of these pieces were left temporarily at a village, Framingham, until the snow was less deep, but General Washington had his artillery, and with it his new, or "Continental", army, which replaced the short-term militia of 1775, and with these elements of force he was prepared to attack Boston.

The British in Boston of course knew the rebels were preparing for trouble, but in early March when an artillery bombardment was begun, Boston's defenders, who had up until then thought the Americans had practically no heavy ordnance, got quite a surprise. It was decided in council to send an expedition against the Americans, but on the night this force – five regiments under Brigadier General Jones – was to embark, "a Hurrycane or terrible sudden storm" arose making it impossible to put men into long boats, and the attack was cancelled.

It was then agreed that Boston had to be evacuated. With American artillerists able to lob shells into the town from the heights at will, and with numerical superiority – or so the British assumed – lying with Washington, General Howe's alternative to disaster appeared to be evacuation.

"The last days of the British army in Boston were days of confusion and distress, of haste and waste, of crooked dealing and actual plundering." What caused this was that General Howe, who had not left Boston earlier because of insufficient transports, still lacked them in March 1776; but he could no longer delay until this situation was remedied. He took all the ordnance he could and had to abandon some. He was also compelled to abandon the cavalry's horses and a considerable amount of supplies, but the loyal Tories suffered worst of all. They had to leave behind entire warehouses and stores with stocked shelves, homes full of valuable furnishings, farms and ships. It was a lamentable leave-taking when General Howe sailed for Halifax, Nova Scotia on 17th March 1776. To add to the jubilation of the Americans who were perennially short of gunpowder, shortly after the British sailed away two royal transports came to Boston, one with a cargo of 1,500 barrels of gunpowder, the other with 700 troops on board. The rebels decoyed both vessels to dock by flying British colours, capturing ships, cargoes, and crewmen.

There was one humorous episode. When it was thought that a contingent of British were still at Charlestown because rebel skirmishers saw redcoated sentries on duty, some bold Americans were sent to test the defences. What they found was that the "Centinels" were scarecrows "dressed in the Soldier Habit with Laced Hats and for a Gorget an Horse Shoe with Paper Ruffles, their Pieces Shouldered [with] fixed Bayonets, with the Inscription wrote on their Breast Welcome Brother Jonathon."

By 20th March Boston, Charlestown and the environs of both were occupied by Americans. General Washington was sure the British were going down to New York and was worried about the result of Howe's landing there with his 11,000 troops and his full complement of Tories. But the British commander sailed northward, not southward. Washington decided to protect New York notwithstanding.

Meanwhile John Burgoyne, appointed Second in Command to Sir Guy Carleton in February 1776, sailed with a force of the German mercenaries — Brunswickers — for Canada in March. That same month Howe abandoned Boston, which was George Washington's first victory of the rebellion — practically a bloodless one. Germain wrote John Burgoyne on 1st March 1776 "I likewise mentioned again the affair of your rank: the King wishes to antedate as far back as you desire . . . so that this point will be settled to your satisfaction." Thus the question of the dating of his commission, which had rankled in Boston where Burgoyne was the junior general, was now settled. Germain also mentioned in concluding this letter, that His Majesty had enquired about the health of Lady Charlotte Burgoyne, so evidently Burgoyne's forebodings about his wife, before he left England, were justified. In fact he never saw her again. She died while he was campaigning in America that same year.

Burgoyne arrived at Quebec near the end of June. With him came the Germans, who were paid for at the rate of 100 crowns annually, plus 30 crowns a head for service in America. Previously, Sir Guy Carleton had been besieged and embattled by the invading Americans under Montgomery and Arnold, but with the fresh troops from Europe Sir Guy's situation was immeasurably improved, and the position of the Americans, which was already deteriorating, became very nearly disastrous.

With Burgoyne and the Germans were seven Irish regiments, one English regiment, and mounds of supplies. Sir Guy, cooped up in the fortifications at Quebec, was suddenly the commander of a very formidable army, and when the news of Burgoyne's arrival reached the Americans they withdrew, at first in an orderly fashion, then, as rumour and panic spread, their retreat became an unprecedented rout.

Burgoyne was sent against two American-held posts: Chambly and St Johns. Fortunately for his soldiers, who were weak and soft after the confinement of shipboard crossing, the Americans abandoned both forts and fled.

The American retreat from Canada was both a wretched and a heroic affair. The ill and wounded were abandoned to die. The lack of discipline (which had never been good) encouraged defeat and desertion, and a raging smallpox epidemic brought down emaciated, demoralised rebels by the score.

The British, pushing hard to overtake the invaders, were occasionally faced by haggard little bands of resisters who sought to buy time for the main segments of the army. Actually, Guy Carleton did not particularly want to force a stand where he might have to take prisoners, and at least once he purposely gave orders that enabled Americans to escape. He did not have any great abundance of supplies; it was both difficult and costly transporting them, and he preferred not to share them with the enemy.

Ultimately, just ten months after the invaders marched north, what remained of them arrived back at Crown Point, the fortification adjacent to Tinconderoga, hoping for safety and a respite. These they got. General Horatio Gates had 9000 effectives at Ticonderoga, and the old fortifications had been much strengthened since the Americans had acquired them. John Burgoyne and another British commander, Major General William Phillips strongly urged an attack, but the American garrisons on the lake were sufficiently respectable to cause Guy Carleton to hesitate, and after considering all factors he declined to inaugurate an assault.

The British did, however, acquire Crown Point, and its American garrison went to swell Gates's garrison at Ticonderoga.

There ensued considerable criticism of Carleton's course. General Phillips, who had arrived in Canada with John Burgoyne, and who had an excellent record as an artillery officer in Europe, was incensed enough at Carleton's hesitancy to write in a letter to John Burgoyne, dated 23rd October 1776, that the atmosphere in the British camp at Crown Point was founded upon "sloth".

He also was critical of the delay, and the apparent unconcern, about a juncture with other British columns in New England by Sir Guy's army. When Carleton declined to attack Ticonderoga, Phillips was disgusted. "I think the army should have moved forward and a trial made at Ticonderoga," he wrote. "Had we failed in a strong feint we could but have retired . . . it is the humour here to suppose that it is no disgrace to retire if it is not done in the face of the enemy." Of the foe, General Phillips, who would die in America, supposedly poisoned, but in any event not very heroically, wrote, "I am and shall ever be of [the] opinion that every art of war should be practised upon these people, whose ignorance renders stratagem surprise so easy to succeed."

General Phillips was energetic and impatient at this stage of his career. Later, he would also procrastinate, but at least in Sir Guy Carleton's defence, when he reconnoitred Ticonderoga and found it capable of withstanding a vigorous attack and siege, his decision not to get involved in a protracted campaign was the right one. October was a bad month to start a campaign. Carleton's line of supply was perilously long, and there was talk of more Americans marching to reinforce Gates at Ticonderoga. Sir Guy withdrew with his army, and in London there was frank disappointment. It did not help much that Lord George Germain was antagonistic to Sir Guy, and as if to give his detractors at home something to be indignant about, when Sir Guy released some 110 American prisoners, including doughty General Waterbury whom he had treated as a guest instead of as a prisoner, giving the Americans food, shoes and a friendly little paternal scolding before sending them on their way, the Ministers at home were incensed. Clearly, Sir Guy was not sufficiently war-like.

General Burgoyne, whose part in the summer and autumn campaign had not been particularly rewarding, viewed six months of inactivity in Canada as anathema. It would not be feasible to start another campaign until the following May; Canada was a poor place, and in London where the planning councils would now undertake to evolve fresh strategy, an enterprising subordinate could more satisfactorily spend the winter.

As usual, Canada's great St Lawrence River was ice-blocked well before Christmas. John Burgoyne sailed for England in

November before that natural condition precluded his escape, and when he arrived in London it was to discover that Lord Germain had decided that since Burgoyne had been with his personal enemy, Carleton, Burgoyne was probably contaminated, and Germain received Burgoyne coldly. But it was always in John Burgoyne's favour that he could overcome enmities of this kind, particularly in men of Germain's stature – colonial secretary and confidant of the King – therefore within a short length of time Germain and Burgoyne were as friendly as before Burgoyne's departure for Canada the previous spring, and Lord George Germain put all blame for the failure to press the advantage at Ticonderoga upon Guy Carleton. This was to overlook the fact that, actually, Carleton's summer and autumn campaign of 1776 had been a solid success.

In general, 1776 had been a rather good year for British arms. General Howe, despite the loss of nearly a thousand of his German mercenaries at Trenton, defeated Washington at Brooklyn Heights, Long Island, in August, and later the Americans were also forced to abandon Manhattan Island, as Howe's desire to control New York's Hudson River and thus divide the colonies moved slowly towards a satisfactory conclusion. By the end of 1776 the notion that America could be subdued by a few thousand troops was no longer a popular idea among either Britain's ministers at home, or her generals in the field, and with the advent of 1777 a number of significant changes were to be made. Even earlier, changes were undertaken. General Howe, for example, who had abandoned Boston in March with approximately 11,000 troops, made his move from New York, to separate the colonies and possibly establish connections with crown forces in Canada in late summer, with a formidable army – 25,000 British troops and 8,000 Germans.

The American Rebellion was finally assuming the respectable proportions of a genuine war.

NINE

General of the Army,
John Burgoyne

From the standpoint of strategy the British position in the early part of 1777 was better than it had ever been. General Howe was in command of New York, a Tory stronghold, and Canada was again entirely under the royal banner. In London there was no longer much credit given the earlier notion that a few thousand regulars marching through some penitent colonies would put an end to the trouble. Elsewhere in America loyal arms under Henry Clinton owned Rhode Island, and for the ensuing three years crown troops lived quite comfortably at Newport, while Tory bands were active elsewhere throughout the colonies as guerrillas.

General Howe wrote Lord Germain near the end of 1776 proposing a vigorous campaign in the spring of 1777 using three corps whose total numbers would be 35,000 men, one corps to carry the war from Rhode Island towards Boston, one corps to neutralise Jersey in order to protect New York from the west, and the third corps to move upriver to Albany in the first leg of a trip designed to effect a juncture with Carleton's command in Canada.

In this same letter, Howe informed Germain that

The enemy, though much depressed at the success of His Majesty's arms, are encouraged by the strongest assurances from their leaders of procuring assistance from foreign Powers, for which end it is understood that Dr Franklin has gone to France to solicit aid from that Court.

I do not presume to point out any way of counteracting him, but were that affected, and the force I have mentioned sent out, it would strike such terror throughout the country that little resistance would be made to the progress of His Majesty's arms in the Provinces of

New England, New York, the Jerseys and Pennsylvania, after a junction of the Northern and Southern armies.

It was the last nine words of the foregoing, reflecting an almost unanimous British view by this time, that were most important. The idea they suggested was the backbone of John Burgoyne's fresh proposal, entitled *Thoughts for Conducting the War from the Side of Canada*, which was submitted to His Majesty through Lord Germain early in 1777.

The King was amenable. Even before he read Burgoyne's plan, the *Morning Chronicle* noted in January that "his Majesty took an outing on horseback in Hyde Park upwards of an hour, attended by General Burgoyne."

As early as January 1777 His Majesty had indicated in a letter to Lord North that he favoured Burgoyne over Sir Guy Carleton when the American war should be actively resumed in the spring. His Majesty also noted "That there is great prejudice, perhaps not unaccompanied with rancour, in a certain breast against Governor Carleton is so manifest . . . that it is a fact."

The King knew his colonial secretary, George Germain, rather well. Also, proving that His Majesty was completely in accord with the strategy of having a British army from the north, and one from the south, join to separate the colonies, the King said in the same letter: "Perhaps Carleton may . . . not [be] so active as might be wished, which may make it advisable to have the part of the Canadian army which *must attempt to join General Howe* led by a more enterprising commander; but since the proposal be to recall Carleton from his government, that would be cruel, and the exigency cannot authorise it. Burgoyne may command the corps to be sent from Canada to Albany."

Subsequently it was alleged that Burgoyne actively sought to replace Carleton as commander of the force to march south from Canada, and yet as early as August 1777, four months *before* Burgoyne returned to London, Lord George Germain noted in a dispatch — that was delayed in delivery — that Carleton was to command only in Canada. Also, while there can be no doubt that Burgoyne's views of General Gage were derogatory, Burgoyne's impression of Sir Guy was entirely different. He defended the summer and autumn campaign of 1776 when any defence of Carleton was unpopular, in public and in private, and long after the rebellion Burgoyne and Carleton remained friends.

Carleton was notified, after a Cabinet Council in London, in March 1777, that he was not to command the southward thrust, by Lord George Germain. "You will be informed that . . . it was His Majesty's pleasure that . . . you should detach Lieutenant General Burgoyne . . . with the remainder of the troops . . . to proceed with all possible expedition to join General Howe"

Upon receipt of this letter Sir Guy tendered his resignation as Governor General of Canada, but when the man who superseded him, John Burgoyne, arrived in Canada for the 1777 campaign, it was noted in Burgoyne's own words, that had Carleton "been acting for himself . . . he could not have shown more indefatigable zeal than he did to comply with and expedite my requisitions and desires."

Sir Guy Carleton was probably fortunate that Burgoyne and not he commanded the southward thrust, although it was quite possible that Sir Guy's very calm, very practical, very pragmatic approach to any campaign might have compelled him to point out the fallacies of this one before leaving Canada.

Burgoyne's *Thoughts*, because they became not only the basis for the 1777 campaign in which he figured most prominently, but were also responsible for the results of that campaign, and had a significant bearing on the entire future war as well, deserve more than passing consideration.

Burgoyne's plan assumed that an energetic British force could push south and join Howe at or near Albany. It did not appear at the outset to expect Howe to send a force northward to aid the army from Canada. The plan also assumed the Americans would be in strength at Ticonderoga. Possibly stronger by three or four thousand more men than Gates had commanded the previous autumn. It called for Burgoyne's force to consist of 8,000 regulars, "1000 or more savages", at least 2,000 Canadians, a respectable contingent of labourers, and "a corps of watermen" or boatmen.

Of this corps Burgoyne was to leave 3000 men to defend Canada. Also, he was to take with him a respectable train of artillery and a considerable contingent of supplies. He meant to re-take Crown Point, which Carleton had abandoned after the previous campaign — another sore point with London — establish a magazine there, attack Fort Ticonderoga, reduce it, and proceed, if possible, by way of Lake George and the Hudson River, to Albany and New York. If the Americans appeared in threatening numbers to contest the Lake George route, Burgoyne would travel by way of Lake Champlain and Skenesboro to the Hudson.

To protect his rear, Burgoyne proposed to establish positions along his route by which his line of communication and, hopefully, supply, might be kept open.

He also suggested an auxiliary expedition, by way of Lake Ontario, Oswego, and the Mohawk River to the Hudson, be inaugurated, with Albany as the objective, and His Majesty approved. This diversionary corps was later put under the command of Colonel Barry St Leger.

The undertaking was ambitious. It was also very courageous in the face of the American Congress having called for 50,000 fresh troops to prosecute the 1777 campaigns. Finally, the entire route to be traversed was through a hilly, forested, ambush-prone primaeval fastness that had no parallel in Burgoyne's experience. It was a watershed that as early as 1642 the French owners of Canada had viewed as the back-door into New England, and for General John Burgoyne its essential value lay in the fact that it was still the back-door into the southerly colonies. Lake Champlain, the Hudson River, the westward-branching Mohawk River, were to be Burgoyne's roadsteads, as were the trails and wagon-ruts over which his boats and wheel-vehicles crossed the mountain barriers that separated the rebellious Atlantic seaboard colonies from the loyal sphere of Canada on the St Laurence. In retrospect one is entitled to wonder what might have been the outcome if Burgoyne, who was energetic, and his splendid force, could have been taken by sea to New York to reinforce William Howe, who was sluggish but who had an even greater force.

It did not happen. What *did* happen was that Lieutenant-General John Burgoyne went *down* that geological fault through the mountain barriers that previous British armies had gone *up*, to conquer Canada for the crown. He used the waterways and roads, which were particularly suitable for carrying the baggage and artillery of British armies, for transporting the army he was confident would secure him glory, position, honour, and a favoured place in history.

But there were always a few anxieties. On 14th May Burgoyne wrote Lord Germain that "The army will fall short of the strength computed in England, and the want of camp equipage, clothing, and many other necessary articles will cause inconvenience. . . ." There had been no new uniforms since the previous year, so the soldiers had cut off their coat-tails for patching material, and appeared now in jackets instead of regulation coats. Not that this really mattered since coat-tails were ridiculous in a primaeval forest, but the point of course was that supplies were not arriving as needed, but this was not new to Burgoyne's expedition, nor, for that matter to the British army in America.

Neither was it unique to Burgoyne's army that the Brunswick dragoons, (who did not manage to see mounted service) set some kind of record for inappropriateness. None of the Germans was properly fitted out for North American service. These dragoons, marching afoot, wore plumed hats, huge gauntlets, leather breeches jack boots reaching well above the knee and weighing 12 pounds a pair, thick, tight coats, and they trailed in the dust of the forest an immense broadsword.

The French-Canadian auxiliaries of Burgoyne's force, who were supposed to number 2,000, and who were described by Burgoyne as "ignorant . . . awkward, disinclined to the service, and spiritless", actually numbered 150.

Of the expected 1,000 warriors, 400 appeared, and of all those thousands of disenfranchised and grieving Tories, 100 stood muster when the army was assembled.

Burgoyne's British advance corps, under Major General William Phillips, was composed of grenadiers and light infantry. His German corps, or left wing, was under the experienced Baron Frederick von Riedesel, who had been gazetted a British major-general. It consisted of the Hesse-Hanau and Prince Frederick regiments, plus a brigade composed of the Rhetz, Specht, and Riedesel regiments, under two subordinate brigadiers, Specht and Gall. The German advance, under Lieutenant Colonel Heinrich Breymann, strengthened by light infantry and grenadiers, was most notable for its special company of *jägers*, German rangers and sharp-shooters, taken from different regiments – a kind of élite unit to counteract the American woodsmen and riflemen.

Burgoyne's artillery complement, which was subsequently

criticised for its size in relation to the rest of his command and the difficult route of travel, consisted of 138 guns including impressive 24-pounders, which were very heavy and awkward to move, as well as small mortars and guns of intermediate sizes. He did not actually transport all these weapons, but from time to time allocated them to positions he thought in need.

Rank and file, German and British, Burgoyne's army orginally numbered 6,740 men. There were also the Tories, the Indians – whose numbers fluctuated constantly – and no less than a thousand camp followers including a horde of women. Official figures gave Burgoyne's number of effectives as 7,213.

It was a valiant, seasoned, tough army. Its officers were excellent men, from von Riedesel who had served in the Brunswick and Hessian armies for twenty years, to Major the Earl of Balcarres, whose valour would shortly stand every test, and Major Acland of the grenadiers whose stentorian profanity when he was wounded, later, would awe the Americans. There was also a bluff, hardy German Lieutenant Colonel, Frederick Baum, who could not "utter one word of English", and a scion of the Scotch house of Lovat, Simon Fraser, whose tenacity was legendary even before he marched south with John Burgoyne. Fraser's corps led the army all the way.

At St Johns, a short distance below Montreal, Burgoyne's campaign opened on 13th June 1777, with appropriate pageantry. A gun salute from the armed transports and shore batteries accompanied the unfurling of the royal standard. Not all the officers were up for it because the previous night General Phillips had been host at a farewell dinner and the liquor had flowed freely. Also, Baron von Riedesel was not on hand on the 13th because his dumpy little Baroness had arrived with their three small daughters. He had been granted a brief leave.

After the gun salute Burgoyne and William Phillips saluted the royal banner and the campaign began. Burgoyne watched as all the regiments were taken aboard his ships. He personally did not go aboard until the 17th, and, once on board the *Lady Maria* – named after Sir Guy Carleton's young wife – General of the Army John Burgoyne composed a *Proclamation to the American People*. In this he said, among other things, that

The forces intrusted to my command are designed to act in concert and upon a common principle with the numerous armies and fleets which already display in every quarter of America the Power, the Justice (and when properly sought) the Mercy of the King. The cause in which the British armies are exerted, applies to the most affecting interest of the human heart, and the military servants of the crown, at first called forth for the sole purpose of Restoring the rights of the Constitution, now combine with love of Country, and duty to their Soverign, the other extensive incitements which spring from a true sense of the general privileges of mankind. To the eyes and ears of the temperate part of the public, and to the breasts of the suffering thousands in the Provinces, be the melancholy appeal, whether the present unnatural Rebellion has not been made a foundation for the completest system of tyranny that ever God in his displeasure suffered for a time to be exercised over a forward and stubborn Generation. Arbitrary Imprisonment, confiscation of property, Persecution and torture unprecedented . . . are amongst the palpable enormities that verify the affirmative.

There was quite a bit more: "The domestic, the industrious, the infirm, and even the timid inhabitants I am desireous to protect." It read, actually, more like the *grito* of some Latin American *pronunciado*. There was also an ominous threat that no American overlooked or forgot. "I have but to give stretch to the Indian forces under my direction . . . to overtake the hardened enemies of Great Britain and [loyal] America."

The American reaction to Burgoyne's coming was to stiffen all resolve. The reaction to his proclamation was anger over the threats, particularly the one about "giving stretch" or turning loose, his savages, but subsequently parodies by the score appeared and eventually amusement replaced the anger. In England, too, the proclamation was ridiculed. Horace Walpole called Burgoyne "Pomposo", and wondered how he could "reconcile the scalping knife with the Gospel", but then Walpole had always been antagonistic towards John Burgoyne.

On 20th June, General Burgoyne addressed a council of Indians, under the aegis of an old man, the Canadian Chevalier St Luc de la Corne, who was powerful and influential in the redskins' lodges, and who was also a traitor when the opportunity presented itself. This time Burgoyne's address got almost unanimous ridicule. He told the Indians the rebellious Americans were "parricides of State."

He gave them permission to wage war against all who had abused the King's clemency. He praised the Indians' loyalty to His Majesty, and then he made a mistake; he forbade the savages to kill non-combatants, women, children, the aged and the ill, or all those who, in the eyes of the Indians, were the fairest of game because they could not strike back. In Indian eyes only a fool would say such a thing. He also agreed to a bounty on scalps, then said that these must only come from the heads of the slain. He also agreed to pay for prisoners, and he said, "I positively forbid bloodshed, when you are not opposed in arms."

To the Indians the handsome and resplendent man in his scarlet coat and lace appeared as a genuine paradox, a genuine example of white-man inconsistency; he forbade on the one hand and offered rewards on the other hand.

Rum was brought ashore after the council was over, the Indians put on a simulated war-dance, to the discomfort of the Europeans, and "every now and then" made "hideous yells". When it was over the Europeans were happy to depart. In the dawn of firstlight on the 21st the Indians were gone, already coursing ahead.

TEN

The First Triumphs

On 25th June, General Fraser's advance corps went ashore to reconnoitre Crown Point, the first enemy outpost. After considerable preparation for an assault some skirmishers got up close enough to discover that the place was deserted.

Twelve miles on down the lake was Ticonderoga. It was reasonably assumed that here the first real contact with hostile Americans would occur. It was essential to Burgoyne's plan that Ticonderoga be in British hands when he continued southward. There would, inevitably, be roving bands of American partisans in Burgoyne's rear the farther he marched into rebel territory, but as long as the principal forts were in friendly hands he could feel moderately secure.

Ticonderoga had been in American hands for two years by this time, and considerable work had been done to strengthen it. For example, across the narrows on the opposite shore had been erected a sturdy installation called Mount Independence. Otherwise, the bold, rather square, blunt promontory itself, which was about a mile long and three-quarters of a mile wide, jutting out from the west side of Lake Champlain, whose waters washed its base on the north, east and west, had been armed so that a British squadron seeking to force passage from Champlain to Lake George, southward, would be caught in a killing grid of gunfire.

The previous year General Horatio Gates, a former British officer, had commanded, but General Philip Schuyler, commander of the northern department under General Washington, had sent another former British officer, Arthur St Clair, an American Major General, to command Ticonderoga in 1777.

St Clair, by birth a Scot, has 2,500 men with which to hold Ticonderoga. The previous year Gates had been fortunate enough to have about five times that many, without being in imminent danger of attack. If St Clair could have been reinforced he might have been able to defend Ticonderoga, but without help, there was never a chance that he could withstand Burgoyne's scarlet wave.

Clearly, Ticonderoga was to be the first test for Burgoyne. He ordered the advance undertaken in the first day of July. General Phillips and the British moved up on the west shore. General von Riedesel and the Germans advanced on the east shore. Between, was Burgoyne's respectable 'navy', with its armament on board and ready.

Scouting Indians reported Americans on ahead in great numbers. Indians as messengers, unless told what to say by experienced scouts, were worthless. An Irishman, lying close and aiming at an unsuspecting American, was seen from the parapet and fired upon. At once gunfire erupted all along the parapets. The Irishman had missed, and unable to jump up and flee, he played dead, while all the other rangers and Indians departed.

An American patrol came out to examine the 'dead' redcoat, who greeted them with his hands upraised. He was taken prisoner, and no more Americans went beyond the works. General Phillips, using two brigades, enveloped the fort so that no reinforcements could reach it, if any were coming – they were not – and across the narrows von Riedesel's Germans flanked the defences at Mount Independence.

General Burgoyne, who went on horseback to inspect the siege lines, noticed Sugar Loaf Mountain nearby, and asked an artilleryman, Major Griffith Williams, and an engineering subordinate, Lieutenant William Twiss, to ascertain if a gun could be put up there to fire down inside the American fortifications.

Williams and Twiss reported at dusk of 4th July that it would be possible, with much labour, to put guns on the height. All the following day men and horses worked in the humid heat cutting brush, snaking away trees, clearing a road, and at night when it was possible to move up the guns, Burgoyne and Phillips were confident of what would happen the next day, 6th July, 1777.

Gun crews worked at assembling their cannon on the night of 5th July under a weak moon and a million stars, but earlier, about sundown or shortly before, the anxious Americans, who could not have avoided knowing their besiegers were up to something, caught the reflection of failing sunlight off British metal on the heights. Shortly after nightfall, St Clair passed quiet orders.

Not long before dawn on 6th July, British sentries roused their officers with word of a fire inside the American lines. While this information was being passed up the chain of command, some British troops on picket duty came into camp with three American deserters who told an electrifying tale: General St Clair and his entire force had slipped away silently in the night, some going southward down the lake by boat, the majority hurrying eastward into the hills towards Hubbardton and the Green Mountains.

Immediately, British scouts were sent out. It was true. Not only were the boats gone, but so were all the supplies which could be carried. Everything else had been smashed or trampled to make it useless.

Inside the fortifications prowling British troopers found one American – dead on an earthen floor and covered by an old blanket.

Generals von Riedesel and Fraser met in the sooty dawn and after dispatching a messenger to General Burgoyne, they awaited permission to start in pursuit. It did not come until well after sun up, by which time the escaping rebels, bred to the mountains and inspired by what lay behind them to make haste, had covered quite a few miles. Eventually Fraser struck out with some grenadiers, a unit of his light infantry, and an element of the 24th foot.

General von Riedesel followed after, but Fraser's contingent made such excellent time that the Germans did not find them until mid-afternoon. Neither contingent of troops had eaten since the previous day, it was breathlessly hot in the forested hills, and except that they found ample water the pursuit probably would have failed.

When Fraser and von Riedesel met in the afternoon and took council, it was decided that the British should continue in the lead, which they did. Still hungry, when they bedded down at dark atop a clear hill they had covered a respectable distance and were a lot closer to the nearest village, Hubbardton, than anyone, including the Americans, had any idea they might be.

At three o'clock the following pre-dawn Fraser's corps was again on the move, Major Robert Grant of the 24th Foot leading the skirmishers down through the hills towards the road that led inland from not far below Ticonderoga, to Hubbardton, kept a smart pace, and suddenly, as the light infantry stepped into a clearing where a watercourse bisected the flat land, Major Grant and his advance elements got a surprise; American soldiers were washing along the creek, while beyond, their regimental comrades were at work unconcernedly cooking breakfast. The last thing either side expected at dawn was the appearance of the other. Major Grant turned to shout an order. An American rifleman dropped to one knee, fired, and Robert Grant fell dead. The redcoats deployed and pressed, forward. The Americans at the creek, many only partially dressed, had no guns at hand. The men at the cooking fires were more readily able to recover and make a stand. These rebels were New Hampshiremen, under Colonel Nathan Hale. It became obvious that they were greatly outnumbered by Fraser's corps, and they were also burdened with a number of ill and injured. Colonel Hale, while seeking to create a defensive rear guard so that the main body of his troops might withdraw, was engulfed when the advancing redcoat ranks, bayonets extended, over-ran his camp. He was captured.

The routed Americans ran into the forest. From there they turned to fire from behind outcroppings of stone, tall trees, anything that presented either concealment or shelter.

The British did not stop in the clearing. General Fraser assumed forward command in an effort to destroy this rear-guard of St Clair's corps so that he might push on and strike the main army at, or near, the village of Castleton, due south on the road from Hubbardton, where it was assumed the Americans had been in bivouac.

The Americans made a stand atop a partially fortified hill and John Acland was sent up with his grenadiers to take it. The climb was steep, Americans peppered the panting, perspiring redcoats, and near the eminence the Americans rushed the grenadiers, who repulsed them, and Major Acland had his hilltop.

The fight became general as the withdrawing Americans stood. General von Riedesel turned the enemy's flank as the British advanced, and the Americans finally yielded. As they fled, occasionally dropping low to snipe, the British and Germans stood fast. They were exhausted, low on ammunition, and it seemed fair to assume that since the Battle of Hubbardton had commenced, rebel reinforcements most surely would be on the way. They were not, but taking that chance was not sensible, so the Americans escaped.

One of the final shots in this engagement occurred after the fighting had ceased and some officers were standing over the corpse of Colonel Ebenezer Francis, commander of the 11th Massachusetts Regiment. Captain Shrimpton was examining the dead man's effects when a rebel marksman fired from among the trees. Captain Shrimpton, hit hard, collapsed across the dead American.

General Burgoyne, thinking to catch the rebels who had fled Ticonderoga by boat, had Colonel John Hill's 9th Regiment of Foot sent overland to the vicinity of Fort Anne where, in conjunction with Colonel Lind and Major Squire of the 20th and 21st regiments, Hill was to drive any rebels he found northward up the road that paralleled Wood Creek towards Skenesboro where they could be met by the 20th and 21st regiments, and pehaps also shelled by the ships sent to sink any rebel boats found at Skenesboro, which was where the Americans had created their vessels the year before with which they held up Carleton's southward thrust.

The armed ships found a number of rebel vessels including two warships, which were blown up. They also took all the supplies and baggage the Americans abandoned. Skenesboro, seat of Major Philip Skene, the Loyal American now with Burgoyne, had been in American hands since 1775, but by the time Colonel Hill's 9th Foot marched through heading towards Fort Anne about ten miles beyond on Wood Creek and near the Fort Edward Road, Skenesboro had become Loyal again. The major's baronial stone mansion was already being readied as British headquarters.

More to the point, Colonel Hill and his mountain-climbing troops found no rebels. The Royal Artillery's gunboats had scattered them very effectively before Hill's units got within sighting distance of the village.

On the night of 7th July, Colonel Hill's troops were a full day's march below Skenesboro and a mile from Fort Anne, which was in American hands, and was an outpost, actually, more than a fort. It rained the night of the 7th, adding nothing in the way of delight to the hardships the 9th Regiment had borne since leaving the area of Ticonderoga.

At breakfast time on the 8th July, the only time of day when it was too cool for the gnats and mosquitoes to arrive at the bivouac in hordes, an American deserter appeared, to be fed and interrogated. From this man Colonel Hill learned that the garrison at Fort Anne, Long's New Hampshiremen, had been reinforced by Van Rensselaer's New York regiment, making the defending force one thousand strong.

Colonel Hill promptly wrote a report of all this to General Burgoyne at Skenesboro, and scarcely had the messenger departed than Hill's picket line out front sent back word that the Americans were forming outside their elevated earthworks. They then began a very un-soldierly advance, calling back and forth to one another as they came on, moving as individuals rather than as squads or platoons. The watching Britons were amazed and amused. When Hill's pickets fired the Americans yielded temporarily, then came on again, this time with Colonel Long's blue-and-buff uniformed Continentals advancing in line, with banners and fixed bayonets.

Colonel Hill's outnumbered 9th created a log, earth, mud and brush revetment and got behind it, waiting. The Continentals, not a thousand strong as the vanished 'deserter' had reported, but only half that number, pressed the attack, and Hill's troopers, half the enemy's strength, rose up and volley-fired, then charged. The Americans faded into the underbrush but not before the 9th had a string of captives, and the two banners.

Colonel Hill, a middle-aged career soldier, was listening to the rebel's rifles. By that sound he knew the enemy was slipping around to flank him. The Americans were experienced at forest fighting. They captured a number of Hill's men when no-one expected a rebel to be anywhere nearby. They took the surgeon while he was trying desperately to tie off a severed groin artery of Captain William Montgomery, who had commanded the British left. They also got Montgomery, who fainted just as the Americans walked up.

Colonel Hill's cause was lost. There was a growing shortage of ammunition, to make matters worse, and overhead storm clouds as coarse and black as original sin were billowing up into thunderheads.

A spine-chilling Indian war cry sounded back up the road

towards Skenesboro. It rang keening out through the damp and
muddy woods bringing hope to the desperate 9th and bringing
the Americans up short. It sounded again. The Americans knew
of Burgoyne's savages. They began to withdraw, and one of
those events dear to the hearts of Englishmen occurred. There
was no coursing band of scalp-hunting Indians. After the firing
ceased, as the Americans hastened back towards Fort Anne –
which they fired – a solitary British officer, carrying his red coat
over one arm because it was so humid and hot, came strolling
down the road. Colonel Hill met this smiling stroller in the
centre of the road looking for the redskins who had saved him.
The officer threw back his head and let loose a perfect emulation
of a war-cry. He had, he said, started out from Skenesboro with
some savages, but when they got close enough to hear the fury of
the fire-fight up ahead, in the underbush, they had refused to go
any closer, so the officer had come on alone.

It began to rain again. By evening, when General Phillips
arrived with artillery and two regiments, all the 9th needed was
transport back to Skenesboro for its casualties.

Thus far the British thrust had demonstrated great vigour and
strength. In Philadelphia, where the Congress heard of the fall of
Fort Ticonderoga, George Washington's implacable foe John
Adams said acidly that "We'll never be able to defend a post
until we shoot a general," and the friends of General Gates –
another former British officer – who aspired to full command in
the north, exerted pressure through the Congress to make
Washington replace his friend, Philip Schuyler, with Gates. It
had been Schuyler who had put St Clair in command at Ticonderoga, and that, in American minds, had been the beginning of
the whole sequence of disasters.

The loss of Skenesboro was another blow, not of the same
magnitude, because Ticonderoga was a symbol, having been the
first fort taken from the British after the opening of hostilities,
but when the loss on the lake was coupled with the abandonment
of Skenesboro and the destruction of Fort Anne, there was much
cause for demoralisation – and censure – among the
Americans.

Eventually General Schuyler *was* replaced by General Gates,
but actually neither of these officers were of the calibre needed to
face John Burgoyne's disciplined army, which had thus far

advanced at the rate of about eighteen or twenty miles a day, and
was exhibiting a very unsettling confidence, having scattered the
Americans at every meeting while, somewhat ominously,
moving deeper into the primaeval treachery of the American
vastness, the *jägers* in green, the jack-booted dragons in pale blue,
the German infantry in dark blue, and of course the backbone of
Burgoyne's force, the British, in red.

Burgoyne, at Skenesboro with his adviser, Major Skene, his
staff, and recently-acquired mistress, the wife of a commissary
official, was comfortable, since among the baggage was his own
furniture, together with an elegant mess kit containing china,
crystal and a silver service.

It evidently did not trouble the Commanding General that
now, as a result of his fresh victories, he had troops scattered over
a hundred square miles of hostile, mountainous countryside.
Barry St Leger, for example, keeping to his course from Montreal *via* the St Lawrence River to Lake Ontario, then inland
towards a proposed juncture with the main army near Albany,
was making the planned diversion whose purpose had originally
been to relieve the pressure on Burgoyne's front, and was not
only rousing more enemies than he was diverting, but was stirring up the wrong ones. St Leger's force ultimately brought
against John Burgoyne an entire outraged countryside, and in
charge of the converging enemy from the west was the one field
commander who would fight rather than talk or counsel or
lament: General Benedict Arnold.

Burgoyne's position was almost as bad in victory as was the
rebel situation as a result of defeat, and Burgoyne did nothing for
a long time to correct things. At Skenesboro his main column
rested and re-grouped, preparing for the next thrust, but elsewhere his lines were extended and vulnerable. Slowly, the
aggravated enemy was gathering for resistance, and if for some
time yet to come they were lacking in confidence, their numbers and fire-power, and inevitably the inhospitable terrain,
were factors strongly in their favour.

From Skenesboro, Burgoyne had a choice of routes when the
advance was resumed. One route was to return to the lake and
strike out from there by water and road to the Hudson River
at a point a short distance above Fort Edward, an American
position. This route he had said in his "Thoughts" was the

"most expeditious and commodious route to Albany."

The alternate course was to Fort Anne, or the smouldering ruin that was left of it, by way of Wood Creek, then by the same southward route the retreating Americans had used, 16 miles southward to the vicinity of Fort Edward.

He chose this latter route, although he had previously thought it entailed ". . . considerable difficulties", and was sure that there would be a necessity "for a great deal of land-carriage for the artillery, provisions, &c."

His reason for taking the direct route was based on something he had said before leaving Canada. "This army must not retreat." At Skenesboro he viewed returning to Ticonderoga as a "retrograde motion", and was of the opinion that it would have a demoralising effect upon his army. At the same time it would encourage the Americans to believe he might be withdrawing from the conquered territory.

There was said to be another reason why Burgoyne chose the difficult and dangerous direct route. Philip Skene, with his 34,000-acre domain restored, needed a road from his village to the Hudson in order that when the war should terminate, victoriously (for Britain of course), his commercial and industrial developments might prosper. As John Burgoyne's local adviser, he therefore suggested that the army move directly southward, creating a good road as it went.

ELEVEN

The Matter of Diversion

The plan had been for a three-pronged campaign. General Burgoyne's unit, striking southward like an axe-blade, was to drive downward through the centre of the American heartland. General Howe, in New York, was to stand poised to strike towards Philadelphia, leaving Henry Clinton in command at New York, with the prospect of one or the other of them going north towards Albany, perhaps, to meet Burgoyne. The third spearhead of the three-pronged 1777 campaign was to go southward from Montreal under Barry St Leger, to make a looping half circle by way of Lake Ontario, Oswego, and the Mohawk River, to meet Burgoyne at Albany.

The purpose of St Leger's drive was to draw away some of the force thought likely to march towards Burgoyne from the vicinity of the Mohawk Valley. But there was more involved than simply a diversion.

The valley of the Mohawk River was the gateway to the western country, and to the land of the powerful Six Nation Indian Confederacy. Britain, committed to the hiring of Indians, and Colonel St Leger, who needed reinforcements and expected to recruit them among the redskin villages, both sought support in the Mohawk Valley which was largely a Loyalist countryside.

St Leger had made good time on his southward course, but there was no reason for him not to since he faced no opposition, other than summer thunderstorms, mosquitoes and mud, all the way from Montreal to Oswego, where he undertook the inland march that was supposed to culminate, eventually, at Albany.

If St Leger's venture were successful, it could have a most satisfactory result, because the Americans, falling back before Burgoyne, might be cut off if St Leger could reach the vicinity of

Albany early enough. With Burgoyne in front, Barry St Leger in back, the rebel army would be effectively blocked, and with Washington occupied watching William Howe at New York, there would be no succour for the trapped Americans.

That was how events might have transpired. How they actually did transpire was different.

The principal defensive post in the Mohawk Valley was star-shaped Fort Stanwix, guarding the wilderness entry to the embattled eastward colonies. Northward ran navigable Wood Creek, eastward the Mohawk River flowed 110 miles to Albany and the populous Hudson Valley. Fort Stanwix, built in 1758 to guard what the Indians called the Great Carrying Place, the portage between the river and the creek, was situated so that it had to be in friendly hands, or anyone coming from the west could not proceed towards Albany on the Hudson. Here, at last, Lieutenant Colonel Barry St Leger, who had come so far unopposed, was to be tested.

For all Barry St Leger's "dashing" appearance, by the time he advanced on Fort Stanwix he was 40 years old and had spent more than half of those years as a soldier. He had been at the siege of Louisburg and the British capture of Quebec. His permanent rank, in the summer of 1777, was Lieutenant Colonel of the 34th Foot, but temporarily he had the rank of brigadier general.

The force originally assigned to him consisted of 100 men from each of the 8th and 34th regiments, 133 Tories, the "Royal Greens", of Sir John Johnson, a great landowner in the Mohawk Valley, as well as a ranger company under Colonel John Butler, another native and influential 'laird' from the Mohawk Valley. There were also some artillerists, about forty in number, and their guns, two 3-pounders, two 6-pounders, and two pair of cohorns, or very small mortars, plus some Canadian labourers and about 350 Hesse-Hanau *jägers*. Altogether, St Leger came down the Ontario waterway with about 875 men. At the Oswego landing he was met by the remarkable Joseph Brant, a full-blooded Mohawk whose sister Molly was Sir John Johnson's morganatic wife. (Sir John, a British baronet, was also a Mohawk chieftain.) With Joseph Brant were about 1,000 Indians. With this force St Leger started out the very next day, 26th July 1777, for

Fort Stanwix, said to be garrisoned by only 60 rebels.

About a week prior to St Leger's arrival at Oswego, Nicholas Herkimer, a general of the Tryon County rebel militia, whose father's name had been Ergheimer when he had migrated from Germany, and who owned extensive farm lands in the Mohawk Valley, sent forth a call to all able-bodied rebels between the ages of 16 and 60 to mobilise against the valley's powerful Tories. There were also rumours of the coming of a British force, and the Indians were clearly preparing for war.

At Fort Stanwix, where Barry St Leger expected to find 60 frightened Americans, there were 750 Continentals under year old Colonel Peter Gansvoort, who had been in residence since April, and had been very energetically rebuilding the dilapidated earthwork until, when St Leger appeared before the fort on 2nd August, Stanwix was suitably defensible again.

St Leger, a man of considerable self-esteem, first sought to in-timidate Stanwix's defenders by parading his units, not the least ominous of which was Brant's Iriquois, already known the width and length of the Mohawk Valley as fierce scalp hunters and willing killers of women, children, the aged and the ill. St Leger's second move was to send a flag and a flamboyant written demand for capitulation to the fort's defenders. It was received, and was never answered.

Stanwix's defenders were not downcast; just prior to St Leger's arrival word had come through that General Herkimer was mobilising the militia to march, either to the fort's relief, or to attack the invaders.

This was true. Herkimer had called for the militia to rendez-vous at Fort Dayton, an outpost about thirty miles below Stan-wix, on 30th July. By 4th August General Herkimer had 800 men, some ox-carts to haul his supplies. He began his march to the relief of Gansvoort's fort, where, meanwhile, Colonel St Leger had detailed all but a few hundred of his men to build a road through the forest – 16 miles – back to Lake Ontario, his route of supply and communication. Otherwise, his Indians and some of the *jägers* crept as close as possible to the fort and sniped. They succeeded in wounding a few defenders, but more import-ant, these two or three hundred men kept Gansvoort's 750 defenders inside their fort.

On the march General Herkimer's column was joined by 60

Oneida Indians who volunteered to act as scouts. While moving up, Herkimer sent couriers to tell Gansvoort he was coming, and to fire three cannon shots to signify receipt of this message, and to also be prepared to rush forth from the fort as soon as Herkimer's relief column appeared, and engage the enemy.

On 6th August, having heard no cannon shots from Gansvoort, Herkimer was wary. He and some of his officers got into a bitter dispute. The officers wanted to rush ahead, Herkimer wanted to go very slowly. Herkimer's brother was in one of St Leger's ranger companies, and this was brought up. It was said Herkimer did not want a general engagement, that he was afraid for his brother's fate, and that he was at heart a coward. In the end, Herkimer yielded, mounted his white horse and passed the order to resume the advance.

Colonel St Leger was apprised of the American relief column's approach while it was still about ten miles distant. He undertook immediate steps to receive it, counting on a successful ambuscade to overcome the disparity in numbers. At the same time he sent messengers towards the lake to recall his armed working parties.

Six miles from Fort Stanwix on the river, in the direction of Fort Dayton, was the village of Oriskany. There, the road crossed a wide ravine that was about fifty feet deep with perpendicular sides. There was a muddy stream at the bottom of the ravine, much tangled undergrowth, and considerable timber. Here, St Leger sent John Butler's green-coated Tory rangers, and Joseph Brant's Iriquois. They established an ambush, with the rangers along the western side of the ravine, and the Indians positioned to cut Herkimer's column off should a retreat be undertaken.

The Tryon County militia marched to the rendezvous, ox-carts in the rear, General Herkimer up front on his white horse, his Oneida scouts completely missing the ambush. The lead units went down into the ravine and started up the far side. Brant's Iriquois sprang up and opened fire, then rushed the stunned militiamen with knives and axes in hand.

General Herkimer's white horse fell dead. Herkimer was severely wounded and lay in the middle of the noisy ravine while his men made for cover. The dust rose in clouds and although the rebels had been caught completely unawares, they rallied so well, forming little groups facing outward, that most of Brant's Indians were frustrated in their scalping endeavours.

General Herkimer was carried to safety, placed astride his saddle with his back to a tree, and as he filled and lit his pipe and called orders and directions, the fight raged on all sides. Then a bizarre event occurred. A sudden thunderstorm erupted, drenching everyone, but more important, dampening the gunpowder, and for an hour, or until the downpour ceased and the combatants could pour dry powder to their pans, not a gunshot sounded, and no fighting took place.

During this respite the Americans paired off – each protecting another's back while facing the enemy from whatever cover was available. Brant's Iriquois took severe losses when they tried to charge one of these pairs after a musket was discharged, hoping to be able to tomahawk a militiaman before he could reload, only to be shot by the other member of the team. The Indians were warriors rather than soldiers. As time passed and the opportunity to massacre the Americans faded, Brant's Iriquois became restless and dissatisfied. They began to depart singly and in small groups. No amount of persuasion could induce them to remain. The Tories, unable to oppose Herkimer's militia alone, also withdrew, leaving the badly mauled Americans in their steamy, humid ravine.

Four days later Nicholas Herkimer died of the body wound he got at Oriskany.

During the Oriskany fight, and before St Leger's summoned troops returned along the road they were constructing, 250 men under Marinus Willett marched out of Fort Stanwix and attacked the camp of St Leger's Canadians and Tories, systematically loading wagons with everything worth taking and destroying all else. When these men struck the Indian encampment shrieking squaws fled in all directions. Sir John Johnson also fled, in his shirt sleeves and bare feet.

Willett's men even tore the hides from the Indians' tipis. In all, Willett's unit got back inside their fort with Sir John's desk, private papers and wardrobe, plus 21 wagonloads of provisions, muskets, weapons of all kinds, ammunition, clothing, Indian packs, and five flags. These banners were displayed from the upper palisades, not far from but lower than the American flag. This was first flown against an enemy from the parapet of Fort Stanwix.

The resistance to Willett's sortie had been negligible. There had been a few regulars in camp, but like the squaws, they prudently, although not as noisily, withdrew. The fact that they put up no resistance was confirmed by the fact that Willett's unit did not suffer a single casualty.

The night of 6th August was full of discontent. Not only had the Indians been deprived of a big kill at Oriskany, but they had lost some warriors, and when they returned to camp, it was to discover that their tipis had been stripped and plundered.

Herkimer's militiamen were withdrawing with their wounded commander slung in a blanket. If they were the last to leave the field and therefore, according to most regulations, the victors, at Oriskany, neither St Leger nor subsequent historians called them that.

All in all, on the night of the 6th St Leger, his officers and regulars were wet, tired, and very conscious of the bitter wailing coming from the Iriquois encampment.

The siege was resumed, although after the events of the 6th it was not as zealously undertaken as before. The Indians were exasperated and talked of going home. St Leger's regulars were suffering from their first decline in morale since leaving Canada, and if they, and their officers, had known that reinforcements were on the way for the Americans, and that this time an ambush would not be enough, they would have had even more cause to lament. As it was, Colonel St Leger sent three officers under a flag to call for a parley. The Americans had the officers blindfolded and brought to a darkened room inside the fort. There, the British Major Ancron said that the Indians were "very numerous and exasperated" over their recent losses, which included several war-leaders, and unless Stanwix's defenders surrendered at once, Colonel St Leger could not prevent the savages from laying waste the entire valley and butchering all the men, women, and children in it.

Marinus Willett answered. "Do I understand you, sir? I think you say you came from a British colonel . . . and by your uniform you appear to be an officer in the British service. . . . You come from a British colonel . . . to tell us that if . . . [we] . . . do not deliver up the garrison, he will send his Indians to murder our women and children." Willett told Major Ancron he had brought a message degrading for any British officer to send, and disreputable for any British officer to carry, and that when he left Fort Stanwix "—you may turn around and look at its outside, but never expect to come in again, unless you come as a prisoner."

Subsequently, the Tory officers who led the Indians wrote a proclamation to the valley's uneasy inhabitants: if the Stanwix defenders adhered to their "mulish obstinancy," the Indians would put "every soul to death – not only the garrison, but the whole country – without any regard to age, sex, or friends; for which reason it has become your indispensible duty to send a deputation of your principal people to oblige them immediately to what, in a very little time, they must be forced – the surrender of the garrison – in which case, we engage, on the faith of Christians, to protect you from the violence of the Indians."

St Leger tightened his siege lines, moved his artillery closer, and began digging trenches that ultimately would enable him to mine the earthworks. At this time Willett and another defender dropped outside the fortifications, miraculously got through the Indians and regulars by night, and after two days of harrowing travel through swamps and hostile country, reached Fort Dayton.

At Stillwater, General Schuyler had heard of the siege of Fort Stanwix and called for volunteers to go to the rescue. The first volunteer was General Benedict Arnold. Such was his popularity that immediately 800 troops agreed to march with him. Arnold left Stillwater on 3rd August. On the 6th, General Herkimer was ambushed. His demoralised stragglers encountered Arnold's marching column later, and were incorporated into it. Also, several recruiters for St Leger were encountered. Arnold appointed a court martial, and although Ensign Walter Butler, son of John Butler who was commanding Tory rangers with St Leger, was sentenced to death, Arnold was prevailed upon to send young Butler to Albany as a prisoner instead.

The second recruiter was Hans (or Hons) Yost Schuyler, whose mother was General Herkimer's sister and whose father was Philip Schuyler's cousin. Despite this rebel heritage, Hans Yost and his brother Nicholas were Tories. Hans Yost was a madman. At least his dementia was pronounced in the Indian camps where he and his brother usually lived, and where he was viewed with the uneasy awe Indians commonly demonstrated towards maniacs. But there was reason to believe Hans Yost had a shrewd streak along with his madness; each time his life was endangered, Hans Yost managed to come up with the right answer to save it. Although Arnold's court martial had sentenced him to die, Hans Yost's writhings and lamentations suddenly ceased when General Arnold asked if Hans Yost could devise a way to make St Leger's Indians abandon the redcoat colonel. Hans Yost, the madman who spoke with the Great Spirit, knew exactly how this could be accomplished. Arnold listened, agreed to Hans Yost's idea, but held his brother Nicholas hostage. Having borrowed a gun with which he shot holes in his clothes, Hans Yost left Arnold's camp heading back towards Fort Stanwix, the bullet holes in his clothing to lend substance to the tale he had to tell of his perilous escape from the bloodthirsty and very numerous Americans. Several Oneida Indians accompanied Hans Yost. These Indians were generally sympathetic to the American cause.

Before Hans Yost reached Stanwix two more couriers, Stiles and Pixley, left the fort and slipped past the Indians to reach Arnold. These men carried the tale of St Leger's mining operation, plus the story of the Oriskany disaster. Arnold at once moved out. He had 30 miles to cover, most of it through country as amenable to ambush as any on earth, and in fact St Leger, aware of Arnold's approach, called a council in the early morning of 22nd August for the purpose of deciding where to waylay this second relief column.

On this same day St Leger's Indians were observed to be greatly agitated. Some of them reported that Arnold commanded 3000 men, and this figure increased as the hours passed. Hans Yost was active in the Iriquois camp. The Oneidas who had accompanied the madman showed wampum and told the Iriquois that General Arnold had no quarrel with St Leger's Indians, but that unless they abandoned the redcoats Arnold would exact vengeance. To make all this especially credible, an Oneida who had talked to a bird roosting in a dead tree arrived at the Iriquois camp. The bird had advised immediate flight. The Indians began to dismantle their tipis and disappear into the forest.

Barry St Leger sent for Hans Yost, but the madman repeated his wild tales to the British and when St Leger accused Hans Yost of treachery and treason, and threatened him, the Indians took exception; Hans Yost was gifted and holy in their view. They had no intention of allowing St Leger to harm him.

St Leger then called a council, only to discover that a great many of his Iriquois had already deserted. The remaining warriors insisted that St Leger retreat, and this the Lieutenant Colonel refused to do. The angry, agitated Indians rioted, stole the supply of rum, ran into the woods, plundered the baggage, stole gunpowder, and when St Leger's men turned out to defend themselves, the Iriquois turned on them, and, as Barry St Leger said, became "more dreadful than the enemy."

When the regulars sought cover in the forest, whooping Indians attacked them, and although they could make no great advance until they began crying out that Arnold's men were rushing the forest, that warning inspired the embattled and confused regulars to break and run, and then they could be shot and scalped almost at leisure.

Fort Stanwix's defenders, thoroughly baffled, could see nothing of the forest fight although they heard shooting and war cries. Later there was complete silence. When they had endured that about as long as they could, the defenders shelled St Leger's camp to draw a reply. They got back only silence, so a wary detail crept from the fort. In the plundered, deserted camp they came upon one regular, a bombardier who was an extraordinarily heavy sleeper. He was as puzzled as were the Americans. St Leger's dishes were still on the table in his tent, clothing, even arms, lay exactly where they had been put earlier in the day, but both the British and Indians were gone, their running fight having carried them miles away.

Arnold was still about 20 miles from Fort Stanwix when news reached him of Hans Yost's unparalleled success. Later, the madman himself appeared, smiling broadly, to secure his brother's release.

St Leger's rout was complete. Although the Americans went in pursuit of him, they abandoned the chase when it was learned that he and his mauled survivors, loyal Americans, Germans and Britons, were withdrawing as rapidly as they could.

The results of St Leger's debacle were twofold. His force, as Burgoyne's westerly column destined to reinforce the commanding general at Albany with Indians and recruits from the Tory stronghold of the Mohawk Valley, was now scattered and defeated. This not only encouraged the rebels, but also precluded support for Burgoyne at Albany. Secondly, St Leger's defeat enabled General Arnold to recruit Americans, not only from Fort Stanwix but also down the valley as he marched back towards Stillwater, so that when he returned to Schuyler's headquarters he had about four hundred more men than he had started out with, plus a good quantity of plunder and supplies from St Leger's abandoned camp, and now he and Schuyler — soon to be replaced by Horatio Gates — could face the oncoming major British column with no fear of St Leger appearing in their rear.

TWELVE

The McCrea Affair

Throughout the Rebellion, but very noticeably during Burgoyne's 1777 campaign, out of the many thousands of people involved on both sides, a few relatively unimportant individuals were able to influence events. One was Hans Yost Schuyler at Fort Stanwix; another the sauntering British officer, with his scarlet coat over his arm, at Fort Anne. A third was a girl named Jenny McCrea, the daughter of a Presbyterian minister of New Jersey, who was savagely murdered by Burgoyne's Indians in the last week of July.

When Jenny McCrea's mother died and her father remarried, Jenny travelled to her brother's home in the Hudson River Valley of New York, roughly mid-way between Saratoga and Fort Edward. Jenny's brother was a colonel of New York militia. As news of Burgoyne's destination and advance reached the valley, her brother decided his family would be safer in the town of Albany, which, in those days, was larger than New York City, and moved them there. All but Jenny, who would not go because she was in love with Lieutenant David Jones, a Tory officer on General Fraser's staff of Burgoyne's column. She went instead to the vicinity of Fort Edward, a dilapidated, practically indefensible outpost, and there was welcomed as a houseguest by a cousin of General Simon Fraser, Mrs Sarah Fraser Campbell McNeil, who was also expecting to greet a friend in the British column.

Jenny's fiancé, Lieutenant Jones, had earned British respect and American anathema the previous year, when he had recruited a company in the upper Hudson Valley, ostensibly to help hold Fort Ticonderoga against Carleton and Burgoyne. However he had instead marched his men around Ticonderoga to the British lines where he and his militiamen had enlisted for the King. People around Fort Edward remembered that. After all but a token force of Americans marched away from Fort Edward, and news arrived that Burgoyne's road-building contingent was getting close, those who had lauded David Jones rejoiced, while those who viewed his act as consummate treachery, began to abandon farms, homes, and businesses, with heavy hearts, and to go south on the trail of Philip Schuyler's retreating Continental army.

There was, at this time, a power vacuum around Fort Edward. It was a time of fluid insecurity when neither one side or the other had control. There was no law.

Coursing ahead of Burgoyne's column were the Indians. Scouts, but more accurately plunderers, thieves and murderers, nine of them under a half-breed French Iriquois known by various names including Captain Tommo and Le Loup, had departed from Skenesboro after General Burgoyne had welcomed a fresh contingent of Indians. They had coursed as far southward as the village of South Argyle by 26th July. There, Le Loup's band raided the Allen farm where two negro slaves and some six whites, including four children, were killed. This attack aroused the countryside. Settlers recalled General Burgoyne's remark about "giving stretch" to his Indians. Others in this predominantly Scottish area, likened John Burgoyne to Butcher Cumberland and all the diabolical, murderous red-coated Sassenach killers, and those that could, some of whom had been neutral before, slunk away to find and join the Americans.

On the 27th, Le Loup and his band was back at the British camp, with their plunder from the Allen farm, safe from an aroused country-side southward around Fort Edward, their Allen-farm foray having presaged an even more notorious crime: the murder of Jenny McCrea.

Prior to Le Loup's attack on the Allen farm, and aware he would shortly be at Fort Edward, Lieutenant Jones had sent a letter to Jenny McCrea suggesting she meet him at Fort Edward, at the McNeil house. Later, fearful of conditions in the Fort Edward area, David Jones decided to send a trustworthy Indian, Duluth, to find Jenny and escort her northward to the protection of the British column.

It was on the same day, 26th July, when Le Loup butchered everyone at the Allen farm, that Duluth appeared at the McNeil residence at Fort Edward bearing David Jones's message for Jenny to come north under Duluth's protection to meet her fiancé with the advancing British column. She agreed to meet Duluth the following day at an abandoned cabin not far from the McNeil residence, in the surrounding hills. Le Loup, resting his band after the Allen massacre, had been watching an American patrol under Lieutenant Van Vechten scouting the hills. Le Loup established an ambush, the Americans walked into it, and the first fatality was Van Vechten who was stripped, scalped, and rolled down a canyon. The surviving Americans fled and the Indians were unable to overtake them.

Jenny, on her way to meet Duluth, hearing the gunfire from this fight, turned back and ran hard for the McNeil house, where others had also heard the firing. The Indians, unable to overtake the American patrol, turned back to track 18-year-old Jenny McCrea to the McNeil house, where Jenny and Polly Hunter, Mrs McNeil's granddaughter, were hiding in the cellar with Mrs McNeil. The Indians raised the trapdoor, saw the terrified girls and herded all three women to the yard where Jenny and Polly were put upon the same horse, but where no amount of boosting, pushing, and straining could get enormous Sarah McNeil on another animal. She was abusively propelled ahead on foot, and the cavalcade started for the British lines.

There were two hidden observers to all this. One was Duluth, who had been alerted by the gunfire earlier, and the other was an American named Albert Baker, who had also seen the death of Lieutenant Van Vechten. Baker had returned to his mountain cabin for some tools, when the scouting Americans had been ambushed. He saw Duluth stride down where Le Loup and his raiders were herding their prisoners.

Le Loup and Duluth discussed Jenny McCrea while the rest of Le Loup's band, with Polly Hunter and Sarah McNeil, went on. In Albert Baker's sight the discussion between the two Indians became an argument. Duluth, sent to personally escort Jenny McCrea northward, intended to do exactly that. Le Loup, the "Wyandot Panther", had Jenny as his hostage and did not propose giving her up.

Suddenly in a fit of towering rage, Le Loup jerked Jenny

McCrea to her feet, swung his tomahawk, and split the girl's skull from the near side. Le Loup then scalped her, stripped her, and kicked the body down into a ravine. He and his friends then hurried on towards the British column.

Duluth went down into the ravine, covered the girl's body with leaves, and also departed. Later, the Albany County militia, the last rebel contingent to depart from Fort Edward before Burgoyne's advance arrived and buried Jenny properly, doing the same for Lieutenant Van Vechten.

Burgoyne's advance was at mess the evening of 26th July when Le Loup brought to camp his ashen hostages, his plunder, and his two soggy scalps, one short-haired, and one long-haired. He showed Van Vechten's scalp to a silent throng of Britons. When he displayed the other scalp, David Jones, although he had not seen his fiancé in a year, recognised her hair, which was "of extraordinary length and beauty . . . darker than a raven's wing." Also, there was the bedraggled and exhausted Sarah McNeil, wrapped decently in one of her kinsman's capes, tongue-lashing General Fraser and even John Burgoyne himself for the horror that had been perpetrated, and she was only the first. The McCrea affair was to work against General John Burgoyne for a long time yet to come, for although Le Loup was the actual murderer, John Burgoyne commanded the savages and the blame was his, and everyone, even Tories, Germans and loyal Britons, saw it that way.

John Burgoyne reacted in anger. He sent for St Luc de la Corne and ordered that Le Loup be taken into custody at once. He angrily directed that a court martial be convened. Upon a number of occasions he had stressed that defenceless people were not to be attacked. He even sent an aide to find a man in the ranks who would have no compunction about acting as a hangman. He felt – in fact he *knew* – that his reputation had suffered; that one of those acts had occurred from whose consequences the person thought to be at fault could not escape, neither now, nor as long as people would remember the inexcusable barbarism itself. At the height of his wrath Simon Fraser, still smarting from what his cousin Sarah McNeil had told him – had *called* him – offered John Burgoyne some very practical advice: put Le Loup to death for waging war in the traditional Indian manner, and the other neolithics would, in bafflement and outrage, abandon

The attack on Bunker's Hill and the burning of Charlestown

An American rifleman, from
*An Impartial History of the
War in America*, 1780

The Royal Marines at Bunker's Hill, from Barnard's
History of England (1790)

the column, which in turn would leave Burgoyne's army, which was getting closer to the safety of Albany every day, at the mercy of American rangers and woods-men, for the rest of the way through the wilderness.

St Luc came in with a more ominous overture for the release of Le Loup: punish him, and as soon as word reached Canada, indignant tribesmen would rebel from one end of the province to the other, to murder, pillage, and devastate, nor could Sir Guy Carleton stop or prevent this because he did not have enough troops. Canada would become a vast charnel house.

General Burgoyne said one thing: he would "rather lose every Indian in his army than connive at their enormities," and he did another: Jenny McCrea's murderer was pardoned, and another Indian parley was announced for the following week on 4th August.

When this meeting was held Burgoyne, a good speaker and an impressive figure in full dress regimentals, left no doubt in savage minds that the McCrea type of thing was not to be tolerated in the future. He tried to mitigate his orders, but beginning the next day, Indians began to depart. Some went back to their villages, disgusted with the white-man's war, but a number of them were drawn like vultures to the fringe of the army, and indiscriminately slew Britons, Germans, Tories, or non-combatants, as opportunity offered, demonstrating that they had never actually recognised much difference between redcoats and all others. This peril of skulking scavengers just beyond the provost lines had one sanguinary benefit, for as long as it was known the savages were out there, desertions dropped to nil.

The Jenny McCrea affair caused a furor among the Americans, who were already incensed over the British importation of vast war parties of redskins. General Horatio Gates wrote John Burgoyne,

That the savages of America should in their warfare mangle and scalp the unhappy prisoners who fall into their hands is neither new nor extraordinary; but that the famous Lieutenant-General Burgoyne, in whom the fine gentleman is united with the soldier and the scholar, should hire the savages of America to scalp Europeans and the descendants of Europeans, nay more, that he should pay a price for each scalp so barbarously taken, is more than will be believed in England until authenticated facts shall in every gazette convince mankind of the truth of this horrid tale. Miss McCrea, a young lady lovely to the sight, of virtuous character and amiable disposition, was . . . carried into the woods, and their [sic] scalped and mangled in a most shocking manner [by] murderers employed by you.

Burgoyne, already upset and sensitive about this affair, answered Gates by saying, among other things, that "I would not be conscious of the acts you presume to impute to me for the whole continent of America, though the wealth of worlds were in its bowels and a paradise on its surface." He then stated the facts as he knew them:

Respecting Miss McCrea, her fall wanted not the tragic display you have laboured to give it, to make it as sincerely abhorred and lamented by me, as it can possibly be by the tenderest of her friends. The fact was no premeditated barbarity, on the contrary two chiefs who had brought her off for the purpose of security, not of violence to her person, disputed who should be her guard, and in a fit of savage passion . . . the unhappy woman became the victim . . . I obliged the Indians to deliver the murderer into my hands . . . he certainly would have suffered an ignominious death, had I not been convinced by circumstances . . . that a pardon . . . would be more efficacious than an execution to prevent similar mischiefs.

In England, public reaction to the McCrea affair was almost as angrily derogatory towards Burgoyne as it was throughout the colonies. Not until 1779, when a lot of great changes had come, did the Earl of Harrington, who had been an officer of the 29th foot under Burgoyne in 1777, say in the committee of the House of Commons that General Burgoyne, although initially very incensed at the murder, had done precisely what he had had to do in order not to alienate all the savages when he had pardoned Le Loup. There the affair rested, but it was never forgotten, nor was John Burgoyne's part in it ever quite condoned.

But in fact Burgoyne's subsequent parley with the Indians, which resulted in nearly all of them deserting him, brought about the very situation he had sought to avoid when heeding Fraser's and St Luc's advice. He could not have suffered very much more if he had hanged Le Loup, an event that every colonist, and even a very respectable percentage of Burgoyne's own troops, would have found entirely satisfactory.

The Indians were a source of constant trouble to Burgoyne

from the first moment they joined his army. They would continue to be troublesome until the end of his campaign. Not only
were they poor soldiers, natural liars and treacherously unpre-
dictable, but in combat they were as likely to shoot redcoats as
rebels. Their greatest value was as scouts, but even in this, as time
passed, special units were developed that could do as good a job
in the forest, and whose valour not to mention their integrity was
superior.

THIRTEEN

To Fort Edward and Beyond

General Burgoyne, while still at Skenesboro, needed word from General Howe below Albany, at New York City, and from Colonel St Leger, to the west. Howe was over two hundred hostile miles southward, and no one was altogether sure where St Leger was. General Burgoyne sent out couriers (not too hopefully, it can be imagined because the Americans had demonstrated an uncanny ability to detect them), but when Burgoyne's road-building, and road clearing crews made the advance towards Fort Edward feasible, and the army was again on the move, Burgoyne sent his messengers southward. He was tantalisingly close to his destination of Albany, but there was information that Schuyler was conscripting far and wide, and that bands of Americans were converging towards Burgoyne's line of march. The rumours that Schuyler was to be replaced by Horatio Gates proved true. Moreover, the Jenny McCrea affair had "... inflamed [the Americans] with such wrath as had not filled their bosoms since the day when all New England had rushed to besiege the enemy in Boston." By mid-August a "sixth of the militia of several counties had marched off to reinforce the Northern army", now under General Gates, in whom the New Englanders had implicit trust; they had never liked nor trusted Philip Schuyler, a New Yorker.

In the Thomas Anburey chronicle of Burgoyne's campaign, under the date of 6th August 1777, and the heading "Camp at Fort Edward," a graphic entry notes a number of worthwhile observations. "We are arrived at this place", says Anburey, whose soldiering for King George had earned him a modest commission, "in which it was thought the enemy would have to make a stand, but upon intelligence of our advancing, they precipitately abandoned it, as they did the garrison of Ticonderoga. . . . The country between our late encampment at Skenesboro and this place was a continuation of woods and creeks, interspersed with deep morasses; and to add to these natural impediments, the enemy had very industriously augmented them by felling immense trees, and various other modes, that it was with the utmost pains and fatigue we could work our way through them."

General Burgoyne's headquarters was established in a comfortable red house on the bank of the river near Fort Edward. Here, his friend, the commissary officer's wife, was made comfortable. Here too, he learned that the Americans had caught two of his messengers to General Howe, and had hanged them. A third courier, taken with a letter signed by Burgoyne, simply dropped from sight. A fourth messenger got through, and returned with a casual note from Sir William Howe, in residence at New York with his mistress, in which Burgoyne was apprised that Howe, commanding general of British forces in the Atlantic Colonies, was not coming north to meet Burgoyne at Albany, but had decided to go south by ship to Pennsylvania which was the seat of American resistance. This left Sir Henry Clinton, commander in New York during Howe's absence, as Burgoyne's possible collaborator. Howe's orders to Clinton were for Sir Henry to act "as occurrence may direct." Henry Clinton, though courageous enough, was a complete mediocrity, a very poor general for an embattled John Burgoyne to have to rely upon.

Burgoyne had expected something much better, and with good reason. Lord George Germain, responsible for Burgoyne's success, had said in one letter to Howe he trusted the commanding General would be able to arrange his schedule so that Howe could ". . . co-operate with the army to proceed [towards him] from Canada." Later, Lord Germain, aware of Burgoyne's lengthening line of supply and communication, and the peril such a tenuous route was certain to entail, wrote specific instructions to Howe for the Commanding General to cooperate with Burgoyne. In a personal letter from Burgoyne to Sir William, written while Burgoyne was still in Canada, there was mention of Burgoyne's orders requiring him to "force the junction" with Howe. In the same letter was the sentence: "But under the present precision of my orders I shall really have no view but that of joining you, nor think myself justified by any temptation to delay the most expeditious means I can find to effect that purpose."

But Sir William wrote Burgoyne at Fort Eward that he was going south with his army, and therefore would not be marching to a juncture at Albany. Clearly, Sir William had not received Lord Germain's explicit instructions, and history has been very kind to Sir William Howe on this score because, in fact, he did *not* receive Germain's letter. Lord Shelburne, quoted in his biography by Lord Fitzmaurice, said that "The inconsistant orders given to Generals Howe and Burgoyne could not be accounted for except in a way which it must be difficult for any person who is not conversant with the negligence of office to comprehend. It might appear incredible but [Lord George Germain] having among other peculiarities a particular aversion to be put out of his way on any occasion . . ." did not sign the orders to Sir William and subsequently went on holiday to Kent, with the disastrous result that the orders were pigeonholed and were not sent to Howe in New York. To this situation has consistently been attributed the débâcle that ensued, and all blame has been put at Germain's door. Granting that Lord George was a difficult man to like or respect, nonetheless his inexcusable negligence in not making certain his orders reached Sir William at New York are only one side of the calamitous error. On the other side was General Howe's positive knowledge that as Burgoyne marched south the Americans were closing in around him. In fact, in the letter that Burgoyne received in early August at Fort Edward wherein Howe announced he would be going to Pennsylvania, he also told Burgoyne that the American northern army was about to be reinforced by 2500 fresh troops. Howe also knew, or his intelligence sources were now totally different from hitherto, that the rebel General Israel Putnam, with 4,000 more troops, was at Peekskill, between Clinton at New York City, and Burgoyne at Fort Edward.

When Howe decided to abandon Burgoyne and go in pursuit of General Washington, it is difficult to imagine how he expected Burgoyne to reach Albany. Howe, was a good soldier, if a sluggish and sporadic one, and may have concluded that Burgoyne's disciplined army would be able to stall and contain Gate's rebel force, at the very least. Howe may also, the first week of August, have thought St Leger would turn up from the west.

In any event, there can be little doubt that, with or without Germain's orders, Sir William Howe must have had some inkling that Burgoyne was marching straight into very serious trouble, and yet he did nothing to make certain Burgoyne would not be badly, even fatally, mauled.

For two weeks Burgoyne maintained his bivouac at Fort Edward. He sent messengers to New York, hoping Clinton might start up the Hudson towards a rendezvous, perhaps at Albany. During those two weeks he had supplies brought down that very long concourse behind him and stored at Fort Edward, which was to be his new base. From Fort Edward he would be supplied on the march to Albany. He had troops guarding his supply line all the way back to Fort George and Ticonderoga, at opposite ends of the lakes, but the biggest headache was transport animals. The horses he had brought from Canada were weak from over-work. Additional teams had been expected, but they had never arrived. While Burgoyne waited at Fort Edward for favourable conditions before going down the last leg of his march to Albany, he had to worry almost as much about horses as about the disconcerting intelligence his scouts and Tory sympathisers brought in about the number of Americans that were beginning to appear between Fort Edward and Albany. It was this lack of draught animals that made Burgoyne's army dependent upon water transport, and therefore unable to leave the Hudson for any length of time.

About the Americans, Burgoyne could do nothing, nor did he expect to have to if he could meet them in battle in anywhere nearly equal numbers, but by mid-August when he was ready to depart from Fort Edward, his over-worked transport animals were in such shape he dared not depend upon them. Colonel Skene, who had previously been so sure that more than enough animals would be available to the conquering army in the upper Hudson Valley, was now equally certain that enough horses could be procured in Vermont's Green Mountains, east of the line of march, near the rich farming area around Manchester.

John Burgoyne, at 55 and as a lieutenant general in command of a splendid army, was a different man from the John Burgoyne who, in Portugal, had blithely divided his force, scattering it far and wide while he rode headlong into the camp of a superior Spanish force waving his sword. Lieutenant General Burgoyne, already beginning to realise there was not going to be any reinforcing column from the west, and very likely none from the south either, was not anxious to divide his force, even though von Riedesel was sure that if there were indeed horses and cattle at Manchester, the Brunswickers would find them, and bring them back.

Burgoyne agreed, finally, to sending the Germans inland. In command of this force – 700 strong – was stocky Lieutenant Colonel Frederick Baum. On 13th August 1777, his negro drummers beat Assembly, just at sunrise. There were *jägers*, dismounted dragoons, Tories, Captain Alexander Fraser's motley crew of scouts. These had very effectively replaced the Indians. Captain Fraser was the general's nephew. There were also German light infantry, grenadiers, a two-gun hitch of artillery, and a sweating aggregate of servants, women, and camp followers, waiting in the heat of a new day for the order to move out. Their first objective was to be Cambridge, fifteen miles from Batten Kill, their point of departure.

General Burgoyne rode down from Fort Edward to see the detachment leave. He still was not happy about this departure. His specific orders to Colonel Baum were to "disconcert the councils of the enemy, to mount the Riedesel's dragoons and to obtain large supplies of cattle, horses and carriages." Baum was to accomplish this while "always bearing in mind that your corps is too valuable to let any considerable loss be hazarded."

Colonel Skene was to accompany Baum, for the purpose, Baum was told "to assist you with his advice, to help you to distinguish the good subjects from the bad, to procure you the best intelligence of the enemy, and to choose those people who are to bring me the accounts of your progress and success."

The country to be invaded extended from Manchester in the north, through Arlington southward to Bennington, as far as the Connecticut River. There was a German band to play the unintelligible and lugubrious marching songs of the Germans, and to remind Americans of the Germans' loyalty to England.

British intelligence knew a rebel regiment under Colonel Seth Warner was in the vicinity of Manchester, but it was logically assumed it would withdraw in the face of Baum's force. What neither the British or Germans knew was that the slow-gathering accumulation that was increasing day by day to face Burgoyne was also active in Vermont.

At Bennington, British intelligence had learned, there was a very extensive and important American depot guarded by about four hundred indifferent soldiers. Here, it was thought, Baum could collect everything needed, even enough horses to mount the suffering dragoons who trudged ponderously through the unnerving August heat, red-faced, blistered, but stoically silent, as the detachment covered its first fifteen miles from Batten Kill, leaving only about thirteen miles to Bennington, much closer than the original target of Manchester.

The first stop was at the village of Cambridge. Here, towards evening, Fraser's scouts, and the Indians who went along like scavengers with every column from either side, captured a few rebel stragglers, but otherwise the village was still, almost empty, with a hush throughout the place.

Colonel Baum ordered his ranks and marched through, his Germans singing one of their gutteral songs, the band playing. People peered from garrets, from behind slats, and from barn lofts.

After supper Colonel Baum, through Colonel Skene and an interpreter, interrogated his prisoners, and made a discovery. Instead of 400 indifferent militiamen guarding the remount and supply depot at Bennington, there were 1800 seasoned Continental soldiers. Baum was not daunted. Like most European professional men-at-arms he had a very low opinion of Americans as soldiers.

Five miles south from Cambridge the Hoosic River ran north to west. Nearby another river, the Walloomsac, flowed eastward from Bennington to a juncture with the Hoosic. Baum's course, by the Albany road, crossed a bridge at a mill named Van Schaick's, and followed the north bank of the Walloomsac to Bennington. At Van Schaick's mill Baum first met the Americans. They numbered 200 men of Colonel Gregg's detachment from John Stark's New Hampshire brigade, which had only arrived at Bennington on 8th August, only three days before Baum's column began its march from the Batten Kill.

It was the tales of Indian atrocities that had encouraged Stark to send Gregg and 200 men to the mill to await the Germans.

There was no thought of Gregg holding Baum. He was simply to delay him. When the column hove into sight the *jägers* were out front and, interestingly enough to the Americans lying in ambush, the *jägers* in their green coats with red facings looked like Seth Warner's men, who had been left back in Manchester.

Part of Colonel Gregg's detachment, including the doughty bridge-builder Eleazer Edgerton of Bennington, were back at the bridge over Little White Creek, three miles closer to Bennington, working at tearing up the planking.

When Baum's Germans got into range, Gregg's men fired a random volley, and at once Baum's *jägers* returned the fire, then broke away to the right and left while a solid mass of blue-coated Germans carrying curved dragoon sabers, charged directly at the mill. Gregg's men fled from the mill down the Bennington road, and while the heat was bad, those grim Germans trotting in pursuit were worse.

The rebels reached the bridge over Little White Creek, got across, and Edgerton's men set fire to what had not already been torn up and hurled into the ravine. When the *jägers* came up they were able to fire a few ineffectual rounds at the disappearing Americans, and to stand helplessly and watch the bridge collapse in a shower of sparks.

It took Baum about an hour to cross Little White Creek, a feat that should have taken a third of that time, and after his wagons, troops and guns were across, Baum, who was an experienced soldier, was justifiably uneasy, because the Walloomsac concourse threaded a narrow valley ideal for ambuscades, a tactic for which the Americans had demonstrated great aptitude. Baum had his scouts and Indians go well ahead.

From Little White Creek onward the invaders móved slowly, both through fear, and because the men had little energy left after their long running skirmish under a pitiless August sun.

Baum, with Skene's help, wrote a dispatch to be carried back to Burgoyne. He had, he reported, acquired flour, potash and wheat at Van Schaick's mill, and although there were somewhere between fifteen and eighteen hundred rebels in Bennington, they would, Baum felt sure "leave at our approach." He would, he said confidently, "fall on the enemy tomorrow early."

John Burgoyne should have had a very bad moment when he read that dispatch. Baum, outnumbered more than two to one, was, quite apart from his personal scorn for the rebels, disregarding Burgoyne's admonition not to let any "considerable loss be hazarded".

There was no ambush, which was encouraging, but some scouts returned to announce that about a mile ahead, across the second bridge over the Walloomsac River dead ahead, the defenders of Bennington had marched out to take up a position, and obviously they meant to fight.

Colonel Baum called a halt, sent a second courier hastening back towards Fort Edward with an appeal for reinforcements, then ordered his ranks for battle.

The Americans that Baum's Tory scouts had assumed composed the entire rebel force from Bennington were John Stark's party, which had marched forth to aid Gregg's men escape. Stark had been informed Baum's *jägers*, Indians, and light infantry were pressing Gregg's contingent very closely. This had been true until the Germans had halted at the ruined bridge, but by the time those reinforcements were sighted across the bend of the Walloomsac, Gregg's men were safely away, and the rescuers were across the river, watching Baum as he came marching closer with his ranks dressed for fighting.

It was too late in the day. The Americans withdrew in the direction of Bennington, Colonel Baum, uneasy down in that gorge, camped for the night on an eminence overlooking the river. He was still several miles from Bennington, and before sundown great, soiled old clouds began piling up, the evening was stiflingly humid, and Baum's men must surely have sensed that rain was on the way.

In the American camp John Stark, with no illusions, sent a rider hastening with orders for Seth Warner to join him at Bennington.

The night of 14th August, aside from being breathlessly close and hot, was full of activity on both sides. Before nightfall Baum disposed his troops to withstand an expected attack at dawn. Stark, on the other side of the Walloomsac, made all preparations to take the initiative on the 15th.

FOURTEEN

The First Battle of Bennington

After the skirmish at Van Schaick's mill, the two armies caught sight of each other about four miles west of Bennington. When Colonel Baum went into bivouac the Americans dropped back to within a mile or two of their town.

The rebel commander, John Stark, was the same lean, indefatigable New Hampshireman who had fought so valiantly at Bunker's Hill two years previously, and whose experience as a soldier went back to service with Rogers' Rangers. He had led his troops into Trenton when Howe's Germans, groggy from a Christmas celebration, were caught unprepared. Although a Continental colonel, Stark, like Arnold, resigned his commission when the Congress promoted junior colonels over his head to become brigadier generals. Thus, shortly before Bennington, John Stark went home, turning his back on the war. But Burgoyne's coming brought him out again, at the behest of his colony, and within several weeks (such was his popularity) he was able to muster something like 25 companies of New Hampshiremen – 1,492 men – ten per cent of all eligible voters in his colony. They were of all ages and carried their own wide variety of weapons. By 7th August, when he was ready to march, Stark decided with Seth Warner, who had been mauled at Hubbardton, to work in concert against Burgoyne's oncoming scarlet wave. As it turned out, however Burgoyne was not coming into New England, but going south towards New York, so Warner remained behind, and Stark went down to Bennington to form part of the accumulation of enemies that were gradually closing in on John Burgoyne.

In 1777, Colonel John Stark was 49 years old, tough as hickory, battle-tested and battle-wise. He was also hostile towards the

Continental Congress, and, like most New Englanders, was sceptical of New Yorkers. He did not care much for General Gates
either, although he strongly believed in George Washington. In
short, Colonel John Stark – commissioned a brigadier general by
the authorities of his colony, but not recognised as being entitled
to that rank by either the Continental Army or the Congress –
dour, sinewy, while a prickly problem to his own countrymen,
was the ideal rebel commander to meet Frederick Baum.

But that meeting was postponed, because on 15th August it
rained incessantly and hard.

Baum's troops, already disposed for battle, did little more than
hunker in wet misery, but across the river Stark's equally sodden
men were cheered by the arrival of reinforcements, some Berk-
shire County volunteers, a war-party of Stockbridge Indians, and
400 Vermont militia.

Seth Warner, riding post-haste in advance of his column from
Manchester, met Stark and joined him in evolving the rebel strategy, and although it was rather complicated for Stark's militia,
it was ultimately accomplished without a mistake. Otherwise,
the 15th was a dull, grey, soggy day. A considerable distance in
Baum's rear, where General Burgoyne had pondered Baum's
appeal for reinforcements, the mud was just as deep when the
order was passed for another German colonel, Heinrich Chris-
toph Breymann, was ordered to march to Bennington and succour Baum, a man whom he disliked. Burgoyne received Baum's
note at nine o'clock in the morning. By ten o'clock Breymann's
Brunswickers, and Hesse-Hanauers were slogging ahead through
the mud.

Colonel Baum's position was excellent. He had clear command
of the bridge and the river, and the narrow passage of the Walloomsac, over which he expected the Americans to attack.
Except of course, that he expected no attack on the 15th because
it was impossible to keep one's powder dry in a driving rain-
storm.

Ninety loyalists under a retired British lieutenant, "Colonel"
Pfister, who had joined Baum, their "uniform" being scraps of
white paper pinned to their hats, were manning an outpost
three-quarters of a mile back, on the road towards Van Schaick's
mill. Closer, Baum's dragoons and half of young Alexander
Fraser's force were posted at their camp on the hill, 300 feet

high, overlooking the bridge a half mile distant. One of Baum's 3-pounders was palisaded there behind felled trees, the other gun, also commanding the bridge, was closer, and was guarded by more of Fraser's rangers, plus about fifty German foot soldiers. The women and non-combatants were herded into some abandoned log cabins out of harm's way.

Colonel Baum inspected his dispositions on the 15th and was satisfied, no doubt, that they were adequate because he made few changes. For a dragoon, Frederick Baum had done a rather competent job as a commander of infantry.

On 16th August, John Stark's move was made, under a grey but rainless sky, over muddy roads and trails; beginning about mid-day, 200 New Hampshiremen under Colonel Moses Nichols undertook an arduous and circuitous march to get around Baum's left. Simultaneously, a force of 300 men, militia from Bennington and Vermont Rangers under Colonel Samuel Herrick, started out on a similar hike to get around Baum's right. Hobart and Stickney, with another 200 men, were to demonstrate against Baum's loyal Americans south of the bridge, while John Stark, with what was left of his 2000 troops, approximately 1300 men, stayed out of sight waiting for the sounds of battle on the German's left and right to disconcert Baum, who would assume these were Stark's major contingents, and would become fully occupied beefing up his wings.

The plan worked, but in a way neither John Stark nor Seth Warner could have foreseen. As the encircling Americans units passed through the woods behind Baum's men, some of them were seen; armed countrymen in shirtsleeves, not keeping any kind of order, and evidently not trying to hide. Colonel Skene, the adviser, had told Baum that this was strong Tory country; that Tories out-numbered rebels five to one. When Baum's pickets reported for instructions, Colonel Baum had the outposts pulled back so that the oncoming countrymen, obviously Tory reinforcements coming to join his column, would not be molested.

The men Baum extended his inadvertent welcome to were Moses Nichols's unit. Herrick, who had crossed the river unchallenged, was already on the road towards Van Schaick's mill and Cambridge, Baum's route of withdrawal.

Nichols's men got close, coolly took position, and let fly a volley that caught the Germans completely off guard. They ducked for cover and Colonel Baum, who was in this area, reacted in shocked surprise, but only momentarily, then ordered all his men to cover. Very gradually gunfire blew up all along Baum's defences. The Americans appeared, not in companies or squads, but as individuals behind trees, stones, folds in the earth. They did not, fire in troop volley, as Baum's men did, but shot individually, and although they were not very good marksmen, their separate, individualised gunfire spattered lead everywhere, rather than in one direction.

Baum, from his hilltop, could have seen Stark and Warren coming from the direction of Bennington with the main muscle of their corps, but there was nothing Baum could do. He was stationary, all his troops were engaged in a sniping fire-fight. Near the bridge the Tories were attacked with great bitterness, and fought savagely. Many of these foemen had been neighbours. When Stark's men stormed over the Tory defences the fighting that followed was unrelenting. Little quarter was given, but when the Tories, exhausted, dazed and decimated, were finally rounded up, told to carry their wounded with them as they were marched away into captivity, it was not an easy thing for the victors to maintain their fury. Too many men were dead.

Baum's Britons and Germans at the Walloomsac bridge were struck with the same fury, and were driven back. As some of these men undertook an additional withdrawal off the Cambridge road, they were staggered again by the fire of Herrick's unit. Some of them turned and dashed straight up the hill past Baum's dug-in *jägers* to the very summit. General Simon Fraser's nephew, ranger-Captain Alexander Fraser was among the men driven up the hill. So was the gun-sergeant of Baum's 3-pounder that had only been fired once when Seth Warner and John Stark appeared on horseback near the bridge. Every other gun tender was either dead or wounded. Only the sergeant survived.

When the Americans swept among Baum's lower defences they captured a log house with some women in it, and in terror a German woman burst out and ran towards the hill. She was killed near the bridge, and lay there in the mud as the Americans hastened past.

Colonel Baum shortened his lines and stubbornly kept his hilltop, but the Americans were drifting in on him from all sides.

His grenadier post down on the route of withdrawl had been taken. He had been completely engaged for two hours now, had lost his cannon, all the lower positions, and was ringed atop his partially cleared and fortified hilltop. His orderly, hand outstretched to receive the colonel's scabbard after Baum had drawn his sword, suddenly went over backwards as the ammunition tumbril exploded. The shock also knocked the Colonel to his hands and knees. It stunned the barricaded defenders, who turned, dumbfounded, to see what fresh catastrophe had arrived, and at that moment Stark's furious charge up the centre came. Americans encircled both wings of Baum's defences on the hilltop. They swarmed over the log and mud-front barricade, some yelling the name of Jenny McCrea, some simply shooting; they caught some of Baum's men still kneeling at their earthworks. The Germans used their swords, and clubbed with their muskets. They tried to form defensive squares and to retreat in order, but the Americans were completely around them. No retreat was possible.

Some enemies, locked together, fell to the ground; others, with useless muskets, seized stones and hurled them. Colonel Baum, thick-bodied, spindly-legged, gathered some sabre-swinging dragoons around him and began a careful, slow retreat towards the downhill slope. For a few moments these men were able to cut a swathe through their tormenters, until Frederick Baum dropped his sabre, shot through the body. He fell heavily, and that was a signal for all resistance to cease.

When Colonel Stark reached Baum's hill, he was told in which direction the few survivors had fled. Americans had gone in pursuit, not only of Baum's Germans and British, but also of his Indians, for whom they had particular ill will. Actually, there were not many survivors. Baum was fatally wounded, and nearly all the other Germans were either dead, wounded or being herded like dazed sheep towards a gathering place.

The Americans looted indiscriminately. They had their pick of weapons, boots and shoes, even clothing. When John Stark learned from his prisoners that reinforcements for Baum were hastening forward, he tried to re-order his ranks with little success at first, and sent word for Warner's regiment to meet him on the road to Van Schaick's mill. Stark, with no idea how many fresh German units might be marching toward him, had reason

Lord North,
second Earl of Guilford

General Burgoyne addressing the Indians at their war feast in
Canada

The British under Burgoyne defeated at the Battle of Saratoga, October 1777, engraved by F. Godefroy after the drawing by Fauvel

to fear being overwhelmed exactly as he had overwhelmed Frederick Baum, and in the same place.

Gradually, as word passed among the looting and sweating Americans that more of Burgoyne's troops were coming, they finally closed up again out of a need for defence. And well they might for of the 642 men being brought up by Colonel Heinrich Breymann, all were veterans taken from the best infantry regiments of von Riedesel's division. Breymann, like Baum, also had two fieldpieces. He was also accompanied by Colonel Philip Skene as advisor, and as usual, Skene's advice was bad.

Breymann's march to Baum's aid was at the rate of a half mile an hour, partly because of the mud but also because his Germans, as usual, marched under full pack. Progress was delayed further because Colonel Breymann, who could not tolerate a sloppy line, frequently halted his troops to have them dress their ranks.

Breymann's guns were 6 pounders. His gunnery officer, Lieutenant Spangenberg, could not keep up. His horses were poor animals, overburdened and additionally harassed by the deep mud. The same condition hampered efforts of exasperated teamsters to keep the ammunition and supply wagons moving. Even on the down-grades it was hard going, and slow as Breymann's infantry moved, the failing horses went slower.

Early on the 16th Colonel Breymann heard garbled reports of the fighting up ahead. Unlike Baum, who had reached Cambridge in good time, Breymann was still seven miles short of it when he went into bivouac on the 15th. Thus the next day he was still at Cambridge when he was most desperately needed at Baum's hilltop.

The weather was better on the morning of the 16th, when Breymann's lines were dressed at dawn, and except for the mud, travel was better too. Although it looked as though it would rain, it did not do so, and was cool until about noon, when the heat gradually increased. By early afternoon it was humid and steaming; men marching under full pack in heavy uniforms got beet-red in the face, their coats turned black from perspiration, and moving one foot after the other required real effort. Breymann kept his men plodding along through the torturous afternoon, and at four o'clock reached the vicinity of Van Schaick's mill — sometimes colloquially referred to as Sancoick's mill — leaving him roughly six more miles to march. Here he heard

more garbled reports of the fighting. At about the same time
John Stark was informed that the second column of Germans was
near the mill, coming steadily onward, dragging two fieldpieces
and a number of ammunition and supply wagons. What Stark
did not know was that Baum had detached Philip Skene with all
Baum's excess teams to Breymann before the Bennington battle,
so that the relief column could make better time. Skene did not
meet Breymann until about two o'clock in the afternoon of the
16th, when it was already too late.

By four o'clock when Breymann reached the mill, Skene and
Major Ferdinand von Barner were already there. Von Barner
was in charge of 80 light infantrymen who, on detached service,
had hastened on ahead. Now, as Colonel Breymann rode up,
von Barner and Phillip Skene were talking to some exhausted
escapees from Baum's battle, and as always, no two men told the
same story. A Briton said Baum was hotly engaged but not in a
desperate situation, while a Tory American survivor said Baum
was fighting for his life. Two German officers, who had possibly
left the fight before Stark's attack up the hill, agreed with the
Briton; Colonel Baum, they thought, was in a hot fight, but was
not desperate.

A lone dragoon of the ranks rode up on a horse ready to drop
and reported Baum's disaster. He was handed over to the provost
guard as a possible coward and deserter. No one believed a word
he had said; he was an enlisted man.

FIFTEEN

The Second Battle
of Bennington, and Beyond

From Van Schaick's mill, Colonel Breymann went forward care-
fully but confidently. He had one advantage Baum had lacked;
Breymann knew there were rebels somewhere on his line of
march who were not going to flee at the sight of a "British"
column.

Still, he made the same mistake as Baum, and for the same
reason. But this time when Skene, riding at Breymann's side in
the van of the relief column, saw the slouching armed men near a
post-and-rider fence that crossed a large clearing where the
column would cross, and assured Breymann they were Tory
loyalists, he got the first shock for his mistake. He booted out his
horse to ride over and accost the countrymen, many of whom
had the white paper patches on their hats Loyalists frequently
affected.

The men at the fence leaned and watched. Two of them took
long rests and to Philip Skene's astonishment fired. His horse
gave a great bound, folded its legs and dropped dead under him.

Instantly, von Barner's light infantry deployed and opened
fire. The lounging rebels were down behind the fence. Colonel
Breymann shouted orders, the big grenadiers formed a company
front, passed muddy Philip Skene near his dead horse, and
Spangenberg's guns wheeled into position on the right side of the
road. The grenadiers, von Rhetz's company, volley-fired, the
usual preliminary before charging with the bayonet, but the
range was far too great for German muskets.

More rebels appeared in small groups. Some deployed for
cover, which was their customary way of fighting. Others
seemed to straggle in several directions as though they were
leaderless. Breymann's horse was shot from under him, as Skene's

horse had been, by these shirt-sleeved countrymen Skene had assured Breymann were loyalists, and as von Barner's light troops swept forward within range, smoke rose from the log fence and infantrymen dropped.

The grenadiers recharged their muskets and volley-fired again, then set their weapons to the fore and advanced, bayonets extended. What probably saved many of those big Germans was the gunsmoke that hung head-high and did not dissipate in the humid breathless late afternoon, hindering accurate shooting.

Colonel Breymann committed more men, Spangenberg's guns were charged and aligned. There was no hope of victory for the rebels anyway – never had been – nor were they supposed to try and halt or contain the relief column, only to delay and harass it, so, before the 6-pounders got the range, the Americans began slipping away. By the time von Barner's skirmish line reached the log fence, the rebels had disappeared back into the nearby forest.

It was getting along towards evening, although as this was late summer the daylight would linger until relatively late. Colonel Breymann, his force regrouped, aligned for the march, gave the order for singing, and his Germans made the forest-shadows echo with their powerful voices. The supply wagons farther back had the assignment of taking up the dead and wounded, adding more weight to the already over-burdened horses.

From the forest the rebels sniped and harassed and bedevilled Breymann's column. Twice, in a fit of black rage, Heinrich Breymann halted, deployed his advance and charged the woods, volley-fired, and scattered the rebels, who, as soon as his panting men were aligned in the road again, slipped back and resumed their harassment.

Breymann was progressing steadily into enemy country, at a time of day when, with visibility diminishing, he might (if he chose not to withdraw back towards safety) have better spent what daylight was left preparing a safe position for the dark hours.

The sniping took a steady, small toll, but it had an unnerving affect. Dead light-infantry and big grenadiers lay at the side of the road as the companies marched past for all to see, until, far behind, came the wagons, and the bodies were flung in.

For John Stark, this harassment was no way to fight, but he

had his reasons. He had got most of the looting scavengers away from the Baum battlefield, but not all of them, and this crippled his corps. Also, if Breymann's red-faced Germans had suffered from the heat and exertion of this day, Stark's men were in worse shape; they had not only fought a savage and exhausting battle, but had been compelled to climb several steep hills in the process and to exert themselves to the fullest, right up until the last shot was fired. Then Stark wanted them to hike back a number of miles and harass another enemy column.

Then there was the matter of German initiative. Every time Stark's rebels decided to stand, the Germans cut loose with one of those senseless volleys of massed fire and came resolutely on despite losses, shoulder-to-shoulder, steel bayonets to the fore reflecting blood-red late-day sunlight. Every time, despite earlier resolutions, the Americans ran into the protective forest where – Breymann was shortly to learn – bayonets were almost as useless as was any attempt to advance a regiment shoulder-to-shoulder.

Also, the militiamen still had a wholesome respect for artillery. When Lieutenant Spangenberg whipped his frothy, spent teams up to wheel his 6-pounders into alignment, dreaded muzzles to the enemy, the Americans went every which way.

Seth Warner's troops, rebel regulars and steady men, were met by the Americans, and Warner had along one of Baum's little 3-pounders. John Stark personally charged the thing while Warner's Continentals set an example for the chary militia, taking a position and holding it as Breymann's cadenced column came on.

The Americans occupied the riverbank and the road. Stark, with the 3-pounder, was on up the road, not close enough to the woods to get away with the fieldpiece if adversity made anything like a speedy withdrawal advisable.

Over three hundred of Seth Warner's men stood easy behind the militia, constituting the American reserve.

Von Barner's light infantry, which had been taking the brunt of the running fight from its beginning, deployed one more time, with its commander attempting by a flanking movement on the right, to buckle the Americans' short and exposed near wing.

Simultaneously with this movement, Lieutenant Spangenberg came up with his guns. Not daring to pass the main German column on the river side because of marshy ground, he wheeled

off on the left. At once rebels in among the trees shot a leading
horse in one gun team very effectively pulling up the other
charging animals, and wounded another horse on the second
gun, making that hitch unmanageable.

Spangenberg had to disengage his guns where they were.
Colonel Skene, rushing forward to help the gun crews, had
another mount shot from under him. He cut out a gun-horse and
mounted it as Lieutenant Spangenberg cried out that he needed
the ammunition wagon at once, and Skene went dashing back
down the road in search of it, while Spangenberg and his gunners, by means of ropes, tried to substitute manpower for horse-
power, and drag their guns into firing position.

As von Barner's infantry, seventy-strong moved to flank
Stark's right, Seth Warner took the reserve, over three hundred
strong and led them at a lope to the right. When von Barner's
men finally succeeded in getting behind some New Hampshire
militiamen, they encountered Warner and were driven back.
This seemed to stiffen the militia's resolve. The Americans
pressed closer and forced Breymann to yield the initiative. His
grenadiers were still firing volley-style, but they did not follow
up with the traditional charge, and as Americans closed in from
all directions, Breymann was compelled to halt, to close up; to
huddle, in fact.

He had not time to wonder whether Frederick Baum could
come to the aid of the column that had been sent to relieve
Baum. There obviously was not going to be any relief; Colonel
Breymann ordered a withdrawal. Von Barner's rangers, nearly
exterminated by Seth Warner's Continentals, were unable to
cover the retreat. Americans overran Lieutenant Spangenberg's
artillery. The Lieutenant was killed between his guns. Von
Barner, with a dreadful chest wound, tried to report to Breymann as the big German grenadiers, like sheep, formed into the
squares they had been taught to believe constituted their best
defence. Rebel riflemen only had to aim into the sweaty blocks
of flesh to score hits. The grenadiers had their ramrods out to
reload for more of those useless volley fusillades, and fell heavily
as they tried to retreat in good order. Stark's men, as inflamed
now as they had been earlier at Baum's hilltop, were merciless.

Day was done. In the bedlam and acrid-scented gloom of
evening two German regiments, those of von Specht and von

Rhetz, stumbled into one another, and in the noise, confusion and panic that ensued, the men stalled, stood and milled, and cried out as Americans shot into them while they were stationary and bewildered. Colonel Breymann, more fortunate than Colonel Baum, while struggling on foot to create order – his horse had been shot from under him earlier – was struck in the leg and knocked down. He regained his feet just in time to see the very thing happen that the entire German system of military drill was designed to prevent – rout and panic.

The grenadiers finally broke. Some flung away their muskets and fled. Some cried for quarter and some raced for the nearest bridge over the Walloomsac, blind to the fact it was in American hands.

Breymann ordered his drummers to beat for a parley. The Americans acted as though they thought that drumming was meant to rally the Germans, and increased the fury of their attack. Breymann, with five bullet-holes in his clothing, limped grimly to the rear to try to organise some semblance of a holding action. What saved him from complete disaster was nightfall, and the fact that the Americans were running low on ammunition. Stark said that "Had day [light] lasted an hour longer, we should have taken the whole body of them."

What was subsequently termed the Battle of Bennington, meaning both engagements, between Stark and Baum, and between Stark and Breymann, dealt John Burgoyne a bad blow. 207 of the Germans were left dead in both fights, 30 officers and nearly 700 soldiers were taken prisoner. The Americans took four brass guns, two 6-pounders, two 3-pounders. They also captured hundreds of muskets, some rifles, almost 300 broadswords, flags, 12 drums, four ammunition wagons, all the teams that survived, and hundreds of regulation bayonets.

About two months after the battle, the same Congressmen who had appointed junior officers to the rank of brigadier general over John Stark, voted him their unanimous thanks, commended his troops, and finally made Stark a general in the Continental Army.

John Burgoyne moved his headquarters down to Fort Miller, to the Duer house, leaving Baron von Riedesel's wife, the Baroness Fredericka, her three small daughters, and her husband's "family", or staff, the red house at Fort Edward. Burgoyne took

his commissary's wife with him. Fort Miller was about four miles
from Saratoga, and was a fair distance northwest of Bennington.
Down the Hudson River from Saratoga were two other notable
places, the nearer to Saratoga was Bemis Heights, the farther was
Stillwater. Thirty miles below Stillwater was John Burgoyne's
destination, Albany. He was getting close. Also, although he had
nearly divided the colonies by his march, that fact was beginning
to appear unimportant. Especially after Bennington. A subtle
feeling, rarely commented on, of plain need to survive, was beginning to replace that earlier proud confidence.

In general orders John Burgoyne noted the effects of the
German defeat, which, had it not occurred, "might have enabled
the Army to proceed without waiting" for supplies from the
north but would now alter his plans "thro the chances of War"
and the troops "must necessarily halt for some days [awaiting]
the Transport of Provisions."

The Bennington débâcle had another unpleasant result. The
Indians who had not left after the Jenny McCrea affair, held a
council among themselves and decided that the redcoats were
not, actually, in too good a position, and that if the Americans
should beat them, the Americans would next turn on the Indians.
The result of this council was that all but 80 of the remaining
Indians packed up and departed.

This loss was viewed among Burgoyne's men with mixed feelings, even after the stunning losses at Bennington when every
musket was valuable. The Indians had never proved themselves
reliable; in fact even when Burgoyne's loyalists and select regulars used as rangers coursed the forests ahead of the columns in
redskin company, they dared not relax their vigil for a moment,
not only because of rebel sharpshooters, but also because their
Indian allies were notorious for killing redcoats too.

Probably the most difficult undertaking for John Burgoyne in
the wake of the Bennington disaster, was the report he had to
send to Lord Germain. In this, lengthy as it was – lengthy as *all*
Burgoyne's writings were – Burgoyne astutely made two worthwhile observations.

I touch with tenderness and with great reluctance points that relate
to the dead, [he wrote] "My defence only compels me to say that
my cautions were not observed, nor the reinforcements advanced

with the alacrity I had the right to expect. The men who commanded in both instances were brave and experienced officers. I have . . .
imputed their failure partly to delusion in respect of the enemy, and
partly to surprise and consequent confusion to the troops. . . . Had
my instructions been followed, or could Mr Breymann (who had
been sent with the Brunswick Chasseurs to support Colonel Baum
have marched at the rate of two miles an hour any given twelve
hours out of the two and thirty, success would probably have
ensued – misfortune would certainly have been avoided. .

These points were well made. They changed nothing, of
course, but they were true.

On 20th August, four days after the Bennington affair, another
letter to Lord George Germain gave a clue to the hovering dark
shadow that troubled John Burgoyne's spirit. He was beginning
to suspect that the fates were aligning against him. St Leger's
silence was ominous. Howe was bound for Philadelphia. Sir
Henry Clinton, left to garrison New York, would not have a
sufficient force to divide it and send part north to Albany, and
the triumphant Americans were probably sufficiently encouraged
now, and reinforced as well, to hazard a pitched battle.

Of his Tories, Burgoyne wrote that he "found daily reason to
doubt the sincerity of the resolution of the professing loyalists. I
have about 400 (but not half of them armed) who may be
depended upon; the rest are trimmers merely actuated by interest." Of general conditions throughout the countryside, he
wrote:

The great bulk of the country is undoubtedly with the Congress, in
principle and in zeal; and their measures are executed with a secrecy
and dispatch that are not to be equalled. Wherever the King's forces
point, militia, to the amount of three or four thousand, assemble in
twenty-four hours; they bring with them their subsistence, &c., and,
the alarm over, they return to their farms. . . . No operation, my
Lord, has yet been undertaken in my favour; the highlands have not
been threatened. The consequence is that [Israel] Putnam had
detached two brigades to Mr Gates, who is now strongly posted
near the mouth of the Mohawk River, with an army superior to
mine in troops of the Congress, and as many militia as he pleases. He
is likewise far from being deficient in artillery. . . .

It is questionable whether Burgoyne's intelligence told him just
how "strongly posted" Gates really was: to oppose Burgoyne's

diminished force Gates had very close to 7000 troops with more coming, at the mouth of the Mohawk, which the Americans did not favour as a battle-ground because it was open country, more suitable to the European style of combat. Once the decision had been made to stand, Gates proposed to move northward, around Stillwater, where the terrain was better adapted to skirmish-style warfare.

Had I a latitude in any orders, [Burgoyne wrote Germain] I should think it my duty to wait in this position, or perhaps as far back as Fort Edward, where any communication with Lake George would be perfectly secure, till some event happened to assist my movement forward; but my orders being positive to 'force a junction with Sir William Howe' I apprehend I am not at liberty to remain inactive longer than shall be necessary to collect twenty-five days' provisions, and to receive the reinforcements of the additional companies, the German drafts and recruits now (and unfortunately only now) on Lake Champlain. The awaiting the arrival of this reinforcement is of indispensable necessity, because from the hour I pass the Hudson River and proceed towards Albany, all safety of communication ceases . . . I mean, my Lord, that by moving soon, though I should meet with insurmountable difficulties to my progress, I shall at least have the chance of fighting my way back to Ticonderoga, but the season a little further advanced, the distance increased, and the march unavoidably tardy, because, surrounded by enemies, a retreat might be shut by impenetrable bars or the elements, and at the same time no possible means of existence left in the country.

When I wrote more confidently, I little foresaw that I was to be left to pursue my own way through such a tract of country, and hosts of foes, without any cooperation from New York. . . I yet do not despond. Should I succeed in forcing my way to Albany, and find that country in a state to subsist my army, I shall think no more of a retreat, but at the worst fortify there and await Sir W. Howe's operations.

Finally, a concerned and grave John Burgoyne wrote: "Whatever my fate, my Lord, I submit my actions to the breast of the King, and to the candid judgement of my profession, when all the motives become public; and I rest in the confidence, that whatever decision may be passed upon my conduct, my good intent will not be questioned."

There was another letter written about this time that shed some light on the fate of the Bennington prisoners. Burgoyne was informed that the Americans treated his Germans, whom they despised as mercenaries, and his Tory loyalists, whom they cordially hated as traitors, much worse than they treated British prisoners, whom they viewed as merely enemies to be bested in battle. In a letter of remonstrance to Major General Gates, Burgoyne said:

> It is with great concern I find myself obliged to add to this application a complaint of the bad treatment the provincial soldiers in the King's service have met with. I have reports upon oath that some of these men were refused quarter after having asked it; I am willing to believe that this was against the order and inclinations of your officers, but it is my part to require an explanation, and to warn you of the horrors of retaliation if such a practice is not in the strongest terms discountenanced and reprehended.

The bad treatment was mitigated, eventually, not as any result of John Burgoyne's veiled threat, but because, as American morale improved, so did the grand feeling of superiority, but this applied to Germans and Britons; for as long as the war lasted, there was no kindness nor sympathy in rebel American hearts for Tory loyalists.

SIXTEEN

Down the Hudson

After the Battle of Bennington all the northern armies became quite lethargic and remained so for almost a month. The cause of the inertia may have been as much the debilitating heat as the fortunes of war. Burgoyne, despite his protestations about being impelled to resume his advance on Albany, which he wrote on 20th August, did not move again until 13th September.

On 4th August Horatio Gates, by "the vote of eleven States," was elected to replace Philip Schuyler. Both these men were American major generals. Gates did not arrive at the juncture of the Mohawk and Hudson Rivers, headquarters of the northern army, until 19th August, that is after the relief of Fort Stanwix, the destruction of St Leger, Burgoyne's right fist, and the triumph over the Germans at Bennington when American morale, as fickle as the springtime wind, had begun to rise again. Benedict Arnold, the friend of both Schuyler and Gates and who was extremely popular with the troops, was also connected with the northern army, and subsequent to his return from the west would play a major role in the fierce days ahead.

Gates, born in Malden, Essex, was 49 years of age in 1777. He was the son of a servant in the household of the Duke of Leeds. He entered the British army at an early age and, by the time he was in his thirties, Gates had achieved the rank of major. He was a very competent administrative officer, and although a brave enough man, was not noted for his battlefield leadership. He was sent to America in 1755 and served well during the French and Indian War. He was wounded at Monongahela while with ill-starred General Braddock. In 1762, Gates, who was an inveterate social-climber, served under Monkton in Martinique, and like Philip Skene, after the war sought through the acquisition of a large landhold to become a country gentleman. In 1775, with the Rebellion overshadowing every other consideration, Gates joined the American cause, was appointed adjutant-general with the rank of brigadier, later served under Washington whom he schemed against, and by 1777 was appointed to succeed Schuyler as commanding general of the Northern Department. His success in the north greatly enhanced Gates's reputation, and for a while history was as kind to him as it was to William Howe. In fact Horatio Gates, called a "kindly and jolly man," was merciless in his machinations against George Washington of whom he was jealous, never overlooked an opportunity to defame Philip Schuyler, was jealous of Benedict Arnold's popularity with the troops, and seldom avoided defaming anyone he thought might become a threat to his position.

Gates's aide, Major James Wilkinson, formerly Arnold's aide but now deputy adjutant-general, was a small, wiry, young, man, devious and treacherous, and almost as unscrupulously ambitious as his commander. He arrived with Gates when Schuyler relinquished command of the Northern Department, in August, 1777. Wilkinson and Gates visited Schuyler in the latter's mansion at Albany, a bitter conference, then went north to examine Gates's legacy, the northern army, for it would be by the effort and sacrifice of this corps that the ambition of Horatio Gates would stand or fall.

Actually, Gates's new command was not yet united at the encampment alongside the Mohawk-Hudson juncture. Arnold, for example, was still on his way back from Stanwix and would not reach camp until fresh battles were imminent. Fat Major General Benjamin Lincoln, who had previously tried to no avail to talk John Stark into joining forces with the northern army, was in Vermont with 500 militia poised to pounce when Burgoyne's flank marched through. John Stark, entreated again to bring his New Hampshiremen to Stillwater and join the Continental army, and who was still antagonistic toward the Congress, declined on the grounds that he had the "meazels" in his ranks. Moreover, the enlistment of his men would expire on 18th September, and if he marched to join Gates his force would arrive just in time to be discharged.

Daniel Morgan, the redoubtable frontiersman in fringed buckskin, sent to reinforce Gates by General Washington arrived in camp leading a contingent of Virginian, Maryland, and Pensylvanian riflemen. Major Henry Dearborn, an American regular and a veteran of Arnold's Kennebec expedition into Canada, was assigned to Morgan with a contingent of 250 young soldiers who were to train, and to act in concert with, Morgan's marksmen.

Gates had inherited a position worth envying: after years of constant manoeuvring, retreating, withdrawing, fading into forests and hiding among New England's mountains, there existed an American army, armed, supplied, and numerous enough to stand in battle. That Horatio Gates had had no hand in creating it did not detract from the fact that, as its new commander, he was in an even better position than was George Washington to face down a *bona fide* British army.

It was also in Gates's favour that, with St Leger vanquished, there was no danger to his flank. Henry Clinton in New York with no more than 4000 regulars posed no threat to Gates's rear, even if he should march – which he eventually would do – because Gates could count on more than enough men to overwhelm Clinton even if he had to divide his force to do it.

At Stillwater on 9th September, a few days before John Burgoyne gave the order that started his columns moving southward again, Gates's chief engineering officer, General Thaddeus Kosciuszko, undertook to devise defences. It was no secret that Burgoyne's destination was Albany, and probably New York afterwards. If he could be stopped at Stillwater it would not only be quite an achievment for Horatio Gates, but a great boost for the cause of independence, and by 1777 American independence badly needed a boost; the French were being courted, and unless America could produce at least one resounding triumph it was improbable that France, much as she wanted to humiliate her ancient foe, England, would form an alliance.

There was talk of reinforcements for Clinton having sailed from England in June. They were due any day at New York. Henry Clinton, whose first responsibility was to hold the city and its vital port, had, on the other hand, been told by Sir William Howe before the latter's departure for Philadelphia, to aid Burgoyne. Clinton's position was not a pleasant one, and while it was true that his city was said to harbour many more Tories, secret and overt, than rebels, Clinton could not take the chance of leaving it. The port, particularly, was too valuable to risk losing.

Clinton's decision, and the right one for him, was to do nothing, pending the arrival of those reinforcements. As events transpired, though, when the troops arrived at New York Harbour after the three-month passage from England, Sir Henry had changed his mind on the basis of alarming news from the north, and struck out with an army 3000 strong in a "desperate attempt" to influence a desperate situation.

When Burgoyne was once more on the march Sir Henry Clinton was not the only one whose perception caused personal uneasiness. Lord George Germain wrote: "I am sorry to find that Burgoyne's campaign is so totally ruined: The best wish I can form is that he may have returned to Ticonderoga without much loss. His private letter to me, 20th of August, contains nothing material about the affair near Bennington, but what alarms me most is that he thinks his orders to go to Albany to force a juncture with Sir William Howe are so positive that he must attempt at all events the obeying of them." Another time Germain said he was "sorry the Canada army will be disappointed in the juncture they expect with Sir William Howe but the more honour for Burgoyne if he does the business without any assistance from New York." But Clinton summed up the opinion in New York quite adequately when he said, "I owe it to truth to say there was not I believe a man in the army except Lord Cornwallis and General Grant who did not reprobate the movement to the southward [of Howe] and see the necessity of a co-operation with General Burgoyne."

Even the Americans were puzzled. It had been assumed Howe would march north. It seemed improbable he would undertake to defeat Washington and try to capture Philadelphia, simply to chase away the rebel Congress, when a British army, much closer to him, was in any real danger.

Lieutenant Anburey, with John Burgoyne's column, said that an American officer who was a prisoner told him Washington dreaded the prospect of Howe marching north to join Burgoyne. Anburey also drew his own conclusions about Howe's going to Philadelphia: "I am too much afraid that those at the head of affairs too implicitly credited every report and are continually led away by false information of men who are interested in the deception and are profitting by the common calamities of England and America." In other words, whoever had advised Sir William to march on Philadelphia probably did so knowing how badly John Burgoyne would shortly need aid. If it appears doubtful that a mere lieutenant of Burgoyne's line would possess that perspicacity, it should be remembered that after Bennington all Burgoyne's troops knew that up ahead was a strong and confident American army, and that elsewhere, east and west, more rebels were moving closer every day.

John Burgoyne started southward again on 13th September. He had sufficient supplies on hand for 30 days. He had sent his ill and wounded back up the long road towards Canada, and now, with a boldness they had not dared evince before, American farmers and woodsmen were banding together to harass Burgoyne's outposts between the lakes and up-state New York. The Indians, former allies of the King, also sniped and plundered when they dared. Clearly, John Burgoyne had stretched his line of supply and communication to its limit. In the first week of September the last of the reinforcements started south from Ticonderoga to join the army, and at about the same time the last shipment of supplies also started south. September in the northern country, as well as along the New England seaboard, was a time of turning leaves, of shortening days, of looking forward to the frost and cold ahead. Early September was a continuation of summer, but later, with cooler nights and brisker days, it brought an end to the period of greatest activity, even for armies.

For John Burgoyne it was more, because as soon as he undertook the march southward towards an insignificant series of bluffs about three miles north of the village of Stillwater, called Bemis Heights, after the owner of a tavern by the river, John Burgoyne was in limbo. Canada might as well have been England. Not only was Montreal miles distant, it was also cut off by bands of hostiles in homespun who drifted in increasing numbers up and down the long trail between the lakes and Fort Edward. It was doubtful, by early September, whether Burgoyne could have got back to Ticonderoga without some hard fighting, if he had felt inclined to make the effort. His best hope was exactly where he planned to march: Albany.

Between his army and Albany, Burgoyne was aware the army of Horatio Gates was digging in. Otherwise he did not know what lay beyond in the 30 miles between Stillwater and Albany. It can be reasonably assumed however, that he earnestly hoped Sir Henry Clinton was down there, marching to meet him, and, with any luck at all, while Burgoyne attacked Gates in front, Sir Henry might strike Gates from the rear.

A messenger appeared, finally, with a letter from Barry St Leger: He was coming as swiftly as possible with his survivors of Stanwix to support Burgoyne. The letter had been written at Oswego on Lake Ontario, about four hundred miles away: Burgoyne had crossed the Hudson on his pontoon bridge on 11th September, and only a few days later was at Bemis Heights; if St Leger had been capable of sprouting wings, neither he nor his unit would have been able to reach Burgoyne in time to take part in the encounter that was steadily and inexorably shaping up. For on 12th September Horatio Gates also moved out, having decided that if there was to be a battle, he liked the area three miles north of Stillwater better. His destination was that same defile of the Hudson, with bluffs on the west, rising abruptly to a height of more than a hundred feet, called Bemis Heights.

Burgoyne had intended to move out on the 11th, but one of those fiercely drenching summer thundershowers had erupted, putting a halt to everything, and on the 12th the river was swollen but passable, the road on the opposite shore was a rutted quagmire, and black flies as well as mosquitos drove men and animals to distraction. Still, Gentleman Johnny Burgoyne stood with his aide, Sir Francis Carr Clarke, on the west side, watching the units cross, enjoying a sight that was bound to stir hope and pride in any general's heart.

The decision to march down the west side of the river was based on necessity. Fort Miller had been on the east side; Gates was blocking the west road at Bemis Heights, and Burgoyne's objective, Albany, would be difficult to reach because the river was wider and more turbulent down there due to its juncture with the Mohawk. Crossing under these circumstances would have been inconvenient at Albany, and surely the Americans would oppose the crossing anywhere, which would add immeasurably to the hazards.

Of course by going down the west road he was going to have to engage the enemy, but that was the purpose of an army, and although Burgoyne now had no more than about 6,000 rank and file, he had reason to believe that Gates did not have many more men, and the Americans lacked discipline. Burgoyne had reason for uneasiness, but only over the unknown. About the things he was sure of, there was cause for hope. Some artillery and troops – 300 of the latter – came into camp shortly before the troops crossed to the west side of the Hudson.

The Germans were the last to cross to the Saratoga road, and on the 15th the pontoon, or boat bridge, was separated into its individual floating sections to accompany the army downriver.

The army marched in three sections: the right wing kept to the right of the road, the left column kept to the land between the road and the river, and the wheeled contingent, guns, wagons, carts, used the road. Because of transport difficulties, that same lack of horses that had plagued Burgoyne from the beginning, much in the way of supplies and baggage went down the river by bateaux.

Altogether, although progress was very slow, the army moved out well. It camped the evening of the 15th at a farm called Dovecote. But on the 16th and 17th, it covered a distance of less than half a dozen miles, although it should have made better time as the ground was becoming harder.

There was no harassment, which was unique. The whereabouts of American armies was usually revealed by groups of sniping riflemen. The closer an enemy got, the more spirited became the sniping.

But Burgoyne knew where his enemy was, athwart the highlands at Bemis Heights. When Burgoyne chose the west bank of the river as his route to Albany, he did so with the full understanding that he was going to fight.

Of course forest-coursing rebel rangers were watching. By the 17th September Burgoyne had no doubt but that "Mr" Gates was being kept informed of Burgoyne's route, numbers, and rate of daily progress.

Benedict Arnold was back with the rebels at Bemis Heights. He and Horatio Gates had had words, and Gates, commanding general, had all but stripped Arnold of his authority. It was a poor time for bickering, but the rebel war effort was never entirely free of this sort of thing.

John Burgoyne had committed himself to three fateful battles when he chose the west bank of the river to travel southward:

Freeman's Farm, Bemis Heights, and Saratoga. The first shots were fired on the 18th, when a number of Burgoyne's men, and their camp-following women, found an untended potato patch at an abandoned farm in an area about four miles north of the entrenched rebels, and went out cheerily to dig potatoes. Americans making a scout approached and fired a volley. They killed several people, captured twenty others, and those who heard the shooting guessed what had happened. Burgoyne got his cue from this, and made preparations to attack on 19th September.

SEVENTEEN

First Blood at Freeman's Farm

Like Horatio Gates, Dan Morgan had served under Braddock back during the French and Indian War, but Morgan had only been a teamster. He was a big, powerful country lad, who now, years later, bore the serrated scars on his back that had much to do with his dislike of the British. An officer had upbraided Morgan during that earlier war, and Morgan had flattened him; for that he had been sentenced to 500 lashes on his bare back.

Dan Morgan's other enemies had also marked him. His face was scarred where an Indian arrowhead had gone through into his mouth.

Morgan had been with Arnold at Quebec. They were close friends. Morgan could have been excused for being sceptical of Gates; no two rebel leaders at the American camp overlooking the Hudson River were as completely different. While Gates went here and there to oversee the digging and palisading, delighted to have endless details to fret over, Dan Morgan went into the hills, stalked one of Burgoyne's few remaining Indians, and returned to camp with a fresh scalp.

The highlands above the bluffs at Bemis Heights rose, in places, 200 and 300 feet above the river, and the escarpments were very steep. There were little ravines, some with running water at their bases, among these bluffs. Mill Creek was one such ravine. It ran north-westerly in front of a position taken by the rebels; it would seriously impair any charge towards the American line.

Another of these broken places, called the Grand Ravine, began in a more northerly location, and angled northwesterly towards the locality it was presumed Burgoyne's troops might occupy.

All this upland country, except for occasional clearings, was heavily wooded. There were trails and wagon tracks through it, some branching off the riverside road Burgoyne had chosen to march down, and running along the uphill slopes to reach the plateau country above.

The main American line was established at the southerly end of the woods, south of Mill Creek, at an elevation of about 200 feet overlooking the river. At Bemis's tavern alongside the river, where two roads met, a trench was dug across the main road, its eastern end anchored where an artillery emplacement was established. Here, Gates also had a blockading bridge of boats swung across the Hudson.

Overlooking this river blockade and accompanying entrenchment, was an earthwork reinforced with logs that formed the culmination of additional defences, including more trenches running at a right angle from the river. This highland fortification, open at the back, had gun emplacements in all three sides. Near this place a farmer named John Neilson had his log barn garrisoned by rebels, who facetiously referred to the barn as "Fort Neilson."

Behind the American defensive line was an eminence that overlooked everything. Some Americans had indifferently begun entrenchments back there, but when the British advance hove into sight on 19th September, there was no-one manning that height. It may not have been the great oversight tacticians subsequently thought it was, because for Burgoyne's troops to reach that hilltop, they would have either to breach the entrenchments or to turn a rebel flank to get there, and if either of those things had been achieved, Gates would have lost the first day's battle anyway.

General Gates's headquarters was "a small hovel, not ten feet square" on a sidehill at the rear of the western side of the highland fortification. There, when he was satisfied everything was in readiness, he went to await the arrival of Gentleman Johnny Burgoyne. It would be a very great day indeed, if the son of a servant of the Duke of Leeds could vanquish a great British lieutenant-general, a friend of a King, the confidant of a Prime Minister, by marriage allied to one of the most influential families in England.

The reason for fortifying all that broken country was obvious.

Burgoyne had artillery and good gun crews. He also had the
ideal martinets for some of those unnerving bayonet advances.
The Americans, unable to entirely off-set Burgoyne's guns, at
least by putting those ravines between the route of advance and
themselves, could seriously hamper the terrible sight of thousands
of marching men, bayonetted muskets to the fore.

Near the Neilson place where a road forked and ran westward
through some oaks and pines, was Freeman's farm. Wagon ruts
ran from here back down to the river, and northward from
Freeman's was the Great Ravine. A road along the north sector
of the Great Ravine junctured with the other set of ruts that ran
between the Neilson farm and the Freeman place.

It was, all in all, a cruel country for infantrymen to wage war
in, twisted, up-ended, bristly with dark woods, rocky and riven
with gorges and mud-hole creek bottoms. But it happened to be
ideal country for Dan Morgan's riflemen, who were trained to
respond to an Indian turkeybone whistle as well as shouted
orders, and it was also favourable to the Continentals, who,
without exception, were hunters who did best among trees and
diggings.

Late on the 18th General Burgoyne supervised the firing of the
evening gun, and so close were the two armies that the sound
carried through the forest, down the river's shadowed gorge, and
across the crystal-clear evening air above the forests, to the American camp. One more night, then battle.

Burgoyne's disposition on the 18th was not changed. General
Simon Fraser, commanding the right, had companies of ten British light infantry regiments under Major, the Earl of Balcarres.
Grenadiers from these same ten regiments were under hard-luck
Major John Dyke Acland, whose pregnant wife Harriet had
trooped the full distance. Acland had been wounded in one of
the fights after leaving the lakes. Although he was now quite
recovered from these injuries, an upset candle had destroyed his
tent and belongings in camp a few nights previously, and now
Acland suffered from burns.

Also with Fraser's wing were what remained of Breymann's
riflemen, and a brigade of guns, four 6-pounders and four 3-
pounders. There were less than a hundred Canadians, several
dozen Indians, and a contingent of Tory loyalists. The total force
was about 2000 rank and file.

Burgoyne's left, under Major General William Phillips and
Baron von Riedesel, was mostly German. There were six companies of the British 47th Regiment to guard the bateaux laden
with critical supplies, but otherwise the left was made up of the
Rhetz, Specht and Riedesel, Brunswick infantry regiments. Also,
there was a German gun battery, the Hesse-Hanau unit of two 3-
pounders and six 6-pounders, 50 survivers of Baum's fatal fight,
mounted dragoons, and some Hesse-Hanau infantry marching
with the carts and wagons, roughly 1100 men.

The centre, under Brigadier General Hamilton, who had formerly commanded the right under General William Phillips,
had six guns, companies from the 20th, 21st, and 62nd British
regiments, with the 9th regiment in reserve. The Lieutenant General was to advance with this column, along with commander of
artillery Major General Griffith Williams.

The army was turned out before dawn on 19th September.
There was frost, but, even less pleasing, a pall of low mist added
to the disgruntlement of men who did not like what they had
seen of the terrain the evening before, in daylight, but who mis-
trusted it even more in a clammy fog.

By pre-arrangement, when everything was in readiness, a gun
was fired. At once the three columns moved out.

The German left marched smartly to band music, but had to
halt several times while engineers went ahead and repaired the
roadbed. The Americans had been busy, as usual, breaking
bridges and creating obstacles. Also, rangers had to be put upon
the heights to protect the column from rebel riflemen.

General Fraser's right wing turned away from the river,
crossed towards the head of the Great Ravine and eventually,
after a tight march, halted west of Freeman's farm in combat
position.

The centre, meanwhile, with an easier course, crossed the
stream at the bottom of the Great Ravine, then halted until they
were level with Fraser, who had had farther to go.

Gunfire broke out, scattered and intermittent, and rebels cling-
ing to the high branches of trees watched all moves the troops of
John Burgoyne made. By heliograph, messages were flashed to
the rear where the generals were waiting.

General von Riedesel got to the highlands overlooking the
river road and halted his column upon a plateau. Somewhere to

the west gunfire brisked up. General von Riedesel sent a courier to John Burgoyne giving the Germans' location and offering help.

Elsewhere, the advancing line of Simon Fraser formed for battle north and west of the centre, where the fighting was in progress. It was the British 9th regiment of Burgoyne's centre that made first contact with the Americans. After high noon when Burgoyne's signal cannon were fired for the second stage of the advance, Gordon Forbes, major of the 9th, led his men through the woods and into the clearing of Freeman's farm. Morgan's riflemen were waiting. Major Forbes led a charge that cleared the farm buildings, but the riflemen only ran into the woods and kept up their firing. Forbes rushed the forest, and it was here, where the Americans were entirely at home, that the 9th took losses. Making matters worse, not only were the rebels behind trees, they were also up in them. Major Forbes ordered withdrawal. The worst was yet to come. As his men broke from the trees another regiment was forming to fire. It had mistaken Forbes's unit for rebels. Major Forbes tried to prevent the firing, failed, and his already thinned ranks took a volley from their friends that further decimated them.

Drummers beat the long roll. British regiments formed on Freeman's meadow. The riflemen who had run into the forest had either gone back to the rebel lines, or were watching in silence from forest-gloom, because now there was no gunfire.

There was three red-coated regiments, bayonets glinting in the afternoon sunlight, formed, aligned, ready to advance, and standing taut. Again the drums rolled, then stopped. Orders cracked. John Burgoyne sat his saddle watching as the red line moved out, guns coming after. Now the drumbeat set a cadence. Now, too, the enemy was sniping again, and although an occasional soldier crumpled, no one heeded. The column's course was towards the trees where the Americans were hastening to form.

Artillery firing canister tore at the trees, and eventually troop-firing by the lines drove the Americans away. Each time they re-formed, however, and now it was not Morgan's buckskin-clad marksmen, but buff-and-blue Yankee regulars, called Continentals, with the riflemen still active over on Simon Fraser's front; each time they fired the sound was different. It also usually meant that either an officer or an artilleryman was down; these were the favourite targets of rebel marksmen.

There was a fair distance between the British 21st Regiment on the right, and Fraser's position, and here the American Major General Benedict Arnold, who had assumed command of the rebel left, struck hard in an attempt to isolate the two separate British columns. He attacked the British centre. As this fight increased in intensity the 21st regiment had to face west to avoid being flanked, which created a salient in Burgoyne's line, leaving the 62nd regiment exposed to attack on both wings. General Fraser sent Breymann's riflemen and the 24th regiment to reinforce the centre, and on the other side General Arnold was strengthened by the arrival of fresh rebel units under Cook, Marshall, Hale, Livingston, Van Cortlandt, Bailey, Jackson, and Wesson, plus Lattimer's regiment on the line.

The clearing at Freeman's farm was about 350 yards long with Burgoyne's guns, originally, commanding all approaches from the northern sector. As the fighting became more savage and determined in this area, Simon Fraser, against whom a probe of riflemen had been made earlier, waited in position on Burgoyne's right, effectively keeping anyone from flanking either the guns or the centre. Here, at point-blank range, Benedict Arnold's Americans fought desperately to split Burgoyne's force. In fact they pushed the red line into the forest, and swarmed over the guns, but, before they could use the guns, a counter attack threw them back. This happened several times. Each time that the British line marched forth, bayonets extended, the Americans fled.

Once the British 62nd, which had been sustaining intolerable casualties, tried to break out with a bayonet charge, over-shot its mark, and lost 25 men as prisoners. At once, General William Phillips, who had come forward from von Riedesel's position to see what was happening at the centre, led the 20th regiment in a bayonet charge, rescued the 62nd, and gave it time to re-form and withdraw. General Phillips also sent to von Riedesel for more guns. All the officers but one, and almost two-thirds of all gunners on the meadow, had been killed or wounded by Yankee snipers, many of whom were up in the trees solely in order to be able to bring down artillerymen and officers.

General Burgoyne's centre was in a bad state. General Arnold, calling for more men so that he would have the added impetus he so desperately needed to shatter the British line, was refused all aid by General Gates until late afternoon, and even then, Gates sent a brigade, not to reinforce Arnold, who was fighting desperately, but to attack Fraser. The brigade was beaten off, and meanwhile von Riedesel, down by the river, decided to go forward to the centre.

He led his own regiment plus several companies of the Rhetz regiment, hit Arnold on the flank and drove the Americans back towards the woods. The Hesse-Hanau 6-pounders were dragged up by hand, positioned in the woods and when they opened up, with canister, at "good pistol-shot distance", the distressed Americans fled.

"The three brave British regiments," said von Riedesel, "had been, by the steady fire of fresh relays of the enemy, thinned down to one-half and now formed a small band surrounded by heaps of dead and wounded."

Von Riedesel had arrived not a moment too soon. As the Americans withdrew – their main line was a mile distant – the British camped on the field, and at day's end the appalling cost was totalled.

Although Burgoyne had had almost 3000 troops in action, only about three regiments in the centre – perhaps 800 men – were continuously engaged. And yet despite this fact, casualties for the entire British force were not less than 600 killed, wounded, or taken prisoner. The 62nd regiment, originally 350 strong, emerged from the first day's fighting with a complement of 60 men fit for duty.

Among the Americans, losses were 64 killed of all ranks, 218 wounded, including 21 officers, and 36 missing. But the biggest American loss was a golden opportunity: while Gates huddled out of harms way with a reserve of 4,000 fresh troops, down along the river where von Riedesel had abandoned all the baggage and supplies for Burgoyne's army, were no more than about 800 men left to protect Burgoyne's sustenance. Gates did not attack, the supplies were left intact, and John Burgoyne retained the means for waging war. He could not have fought even one day more if the Americans had destroyed his supplies.

EIGHTEEN

Bemis Heights

Without the advice of Simon Fraser, John Burgoyne would have attacked the Americans the following morning. It was General Fraser's opinion that the veterans of Freeman's farm were too exhausted, and he was quite correct. In fact he could have been speaking for both sides because the Americans, although elated over the casualties they had inflicted when they fought the King's troops to a standstill, were as battered and bone-weary as were Burgoyne's men, and, lacking comparable discipline, tended to wander from the area.

No food arrived for Burgoyne's men until dawn on the 20th, the day after the battle. Burial details were busy, and, as was the custom, afterwards there was a sale of the effects of the dead departed.

General Burgoyne was at the Freeman house when he received what must have been, to him, great tidings. Sir Henry Clinton was marching north! Except for this news the General's staff could hardly have felt very encouraged, for while they had kept the field the day before, signifying victory, they had been far from sweeping Gates out of the road to Albany. John Burgoyne was being held up very effectively. He had taken irreparable losses, and, granting that many of the troops had not been seriously engaged, it could be assumed that many American troops had not been in action either. In summary, except for the news about Sir Henry, Burgoyne and his fellow generals had cause for anxiety.

On 21st September, Burgoyne sent Sir Henry Clinton a letter urging haste, and outlining the options Burgoyne had of either reaching Albany before the second week of October, or withdrawing back towards the lakes.

Sir Henry's message had been dated 12th September, nine days before it reached Burgoyne. In it Sir Henry said he would be starting up the Hudson "in about ten days." The obvious course for Burgoyne was to do nothing until he learned more, but with dwindling supplies his position was not pleasant. Even if he and Sir Henry forced a juncture and broke the Americans, Burgoyne's troops would still be hungry before they could reach Albany.

The waiting was pleasant for the men until the first week of October when a commissary inventory encouraged Burgoyne to put his army on half rations. There had been a little productive foraging, mostly in corn, but as Gates's soldiers, made bold by Burgoyne's delay, roamed the forests and ravines, it was not healthy for foragers to go very far.

Worse, of course, was the lack of information. If Sir Henry had started from New York on 21st or 22nd September, he should have been in Gates's rear by the first week of October. In fact the distance was not too great for him to have been behind Gates even earlier.

Some Canadian Indians brought news from Ticonderoga: a large force of Americans had attacked the garrison and had been beaten off, but other outposts on Burgoyne's withdrawal route had been taken. Benjamin Lincoln with 1,500 Americans was between Burgoyne and the lakes. Other Americans were infiltrating in force. Withdrawal towards Ticonderoga would be as difficult, perhaps even more difficult, than seizing the initiative and fighting past Gates to Albany.

Time was running out. General Burgoyne held a conference, his second for the same purpose within a space of several days, at which his three divisional commanders, Acting-Brigadier Simon Fraser, Major General von Riedesel, and Major General Phillips, were present, for the purpose of discussing recourses and options.

The plan Burgoyne favoured was not popular with his generals, particularly von Riedesel whose wife and three small daughters were with the army.

The plan was simply to break away with the troops, swing swiftly around Gates and seek a juncture with Sir Henry, abandoning the commissary, all the heavy ordnance, the hospital, and the dependents, meaning the women and other camp-followers.

Von Riedesel countered with the suggestion that the army fall back, consolidate, and await word from Sir Henry before attempting to rush forth and find him. General Phillips was silent, but Simon Fraser sided with von Riedesel. It was too risky, rushing into the forest; even if the Americans could be flanked, suppose Sir Henry was not out there?

Concluding the conference, a compromise was reached. On 7th October, a Tuesday, the army would probe the American left, and if it appeared unshakeable, then the army would return to camp and prepare to retreat towards the lakes by Saturday, but if the Americans seemed weak, an attack would be made the following day, 8th October.

General Burgoyne ordered rum to be issued, twelve barrels for the entire army. He then retired to his quarters to consider a dilemma: where was Sir Henry Clinton?

For Burgoyne's opposite in the American camp, Horatio Gates, the advance of Sir Henry Clinton from New York was small cause for alarm. For one thing, between the engagements at Bennington and Bemis Heights, and the inactivity following the latter engagement, Gates's northern army had grown considerably. In fact, like Burgoyne, Gates had a supply and commissary problem, but he, at least, could successfully forage and commandeer, and providentially, Gates's problem was caused by reinforcements arriving.

The situation of Sir Henry Clinton, meanwhile, who had been reinforced during the last week of September, bringing his total force to about 7,000 men – over 4,000 Germans, not quite 3,000 British – was better by far than it had been immediately after Howe's departure from New York. Thus Sir Henry, 40 years old in the summer of 1777, marched north to create a diversion in Gates's rear, but he never thought it would be possible to reach Burgoyne. As he said in a dispatch to Burgoyne, using metaphor, "You know my good will and are not ignorant of my poverty." Meaning he would do his best to distract the Americans, but could do no more.

He knew John Burgoyne was stalled near Saratoga. On the other side, General Gates knew when Sir Henry struck out for the highlands of the Hudson. He also knew that Israel Putnam with about 1,500 troops, plus two garrisoned forts commanding a gorge of the river, were blocking Sir Henry's way.

On 3rd October, Sir Henry was in Tarrytown, at daybreak,

with two divisions of his corps. He lay over until the following day, until his final column came up-river. On 5th October the entire force took to the river and went as far north as Verplanck's Landing, where a minor American earthwork, mounting two guns, was taken without difficulty. From here Sir Henry struck out in all haste to attack a pair of highland forts, Montgomery and Clinton, and at Doodletown he startled some Americans, who exchanged gunfire with the King's troops, and fled. By half past four in the afternoon, Sir Henry's divided command faced the rebel forts. Two calls to surrender were sent in, and when the Americans refused, Sir Henry's attacks began.

Although American resistance was stubborn, the gunfire sustained and deadly, neither fortification was adequately garrisoned – there were no more that 600 defenders between both works – and both were successfully stormed. By the time this happened it was nearly dark. A great many Americans managed to slip away, including both commanders.

Casualties were especially heavy among the Americans, who had for the most part fought from behind barricades: 200 killed, wounded, or missing, out of 600. Sir Henry's losses were said to be 40 killed, 150 wounded. But this tally was only among British units. German losses, usually reported separately, were not readily available. Sir Henry had Hessians, Anspachers and Brunswickers in his force.

Sir Henry's successes were impressive, colourful, and diversionary. He left troops to garrison the captured forts, sent John Burgoyne a message saying he sincerely hoped "this little success of ours may facilitate your operations" and, having done exactly what he had set out to do, turned about and marched back towards New York.

It did not especially matter that John Burgoyne did not receive Sir Henry's message. He had already decided on his course of action and was embarked upon it when the Americans captured Sir Henry's courier, discovered the note, and disposed of both.

In the relatively quiet period, when Sir Henry was active below Albany, General Gates's 7,000 men had become 11,000, something like 8,300 militiamen, the remainder Continentals, and more men were coming. On 7th October, the date established for Burgoyne's probe along Bemis Heights, the Americans out-numbered Burgoyne by something like two to one. Also, although American ordnance and ammunition was usually deficient, this time it was adequate. Further, the matter of commissary deficiencies had been rather competently overcome, so, while Burgoyne's British redcoats and German bluecoats were trying to stay alive on reduced rations of flour and salt pork, augmented with a little horse meat if the men were not too fastidious – the animals were dying of starvation – the Americans were well-fed and spoiling to fight. In fact, John Burgoyne noted that "from the 20th of September to the 7th of October, the armies were so near that not a night passed without firing . . . no forage party could be made without great detachments to cover it; it was the plan of the enemy to harass the army by constant alarms and their superiority of numbers enabled them to attempt it without fatigue to themselves. . . ."

After daylight on 7th October, Burgoyne's reconnoitring force was mustered. Under Lord Balcarres the right, consisting of light infantry, took position. The left, under, John Acland – whose hands and head were still bandaged from the burns sustained when his tent caught fire – was made up of British grenadiers. The centre consisted of 200 hand-picked Brunswickers, and the British 24th Regiment, under von Riedesel. Ranging ahead were Captain Alexander Fraser's motley *jägers*, Indians, and Tory woodsmen, some Americans, some Canadians, about 600 strong.

A German artillery unit, Captain Pausch and two 6-pound guns, plus Major Griffith Williams and an entire British battery, went forth in support of the three columns when the command to advance was given.

The army moved southwest from Freeman's farm, and after an uncontested advance of slightly less than a mile, the troops deployed in a regimental front – two men to every three or four yards – halted, and sat down in a large clearing while a wheat field ahead was quickly harvested.

American pickets sent word of the British appearance and General Gates directed that two units should advance quietly through the woods and simultaneously attack both British flanks. Dan Morgan was to assault on Burgoyne's right, while Enoch Poor's brigade was to attack the left. This latter force, about 800 Americans, consisting of three New Hampshire regiments, two New York regiments and two Connecticut militia units, had a shorter distance to cover than did Morgan's men, and was engaged by John Acland's grenadiers before Morgan was in position. Acland's men were on a slight elevation and their volley-fire went over the heads of the advancing Americans. Acland ordered the customary bayonet advance, but the Americans opened fire with deadly effect. Among the casualties was the unfortunate John Acland, brought down by shots through both legs. The Americans charged, captured a cannon, turned it on the grenadiers, swept them away and captured Acland, whose profanity awed his captors.

Dan Morgan's men, panting after a hard run over difficult terrain, were met by "severe grape-shot and small arms" fire, but came on steadily, forcing Balcarres to shift position to meet them, and Dearborn's American infantry, in support of Morgan, charged Balcarres's line, broke it, and drove the British back in disorder. Balcarres sacrificed two guns but re-grouped and completed his retreat in good order.

Burgoyne sent Sir Francis Carr Clarke, his aide, to pass the order for a general withdrawal, meaning that the probe was finished. Clarke was shot down and captured, and the fight raged unabated.

The Germans of Burgoyne's centre were attacked by shouting Americans under a burly, dark-complected Continental general officer, Benedict Arnold, but these Brunswickers, recently and hastily reinforced by more Germans – the Hesse-Hanau and Rhetz regiments – repulsed the attackers, and hurled them back. But when Balcarres's force was turned away and the German right was left unsupported, the Americans swarmed forward again, and that time the Germans yielded.

Simon Fraser was personally singled out by General Arnold for execution as he rode his horse up and down in plain sight, encouraging the British and Germans to stand fast. Timothy Murphy, an American rifleman, climbed into a tree on orders from Dan Morgan, and on his third try shot Fraser off his horse, fatally wounding him.

With Fraser's fall Burgoyne's line began a steady withdrawal back to the defences that had been erected subsequent to the fight at Freeman's farm. The Battle of Bemis Heights, which had lasted ten minutes less than one full hour up to this time, was almost finished, and this time it could not be said, by even the most optimistic, that Burgoyne had triumphed.

General Arnold, in one last furious attempt to break the British line, led another charge, this one against Balcarres on the right. A horse was killed under him. Balcarres yielded, and this left Heinrich Breymann, still limping from his defeat at Bennington, exposed. Arnold's Americans overran the German's position, and in the confused fighting Colonel Breymann was shot dead by one of his own men. Here too, General Arnold was brought down by a bullet that broke his thigh bone. He was carried off the field on a litter, lamenting the fact that the bullet had not found his heart instead of his leg.

Darkness closed down. Burgoyne's losses were 600 killed, wounded and captured, and every piece of ordnance that had come into the field with the probing columns.

Gates's losses were about 150 killed, wounded, and missing, but significantly, a fresh contingent, roughly 3,000 strong, had marched into the American encampment near the end of the battle, to join Gates's northern army.

The victor at Bemis Heights was Benedict Arnold. The loser was John Burgoyne. Horatio Gates was a completely superfluous functionary who never appeared on the field, but who remained in his hillside hovel throughout the engagement, a full two miles away.

NINETEEN

Saratoga

The fall of Breymann's position was fatal to Burgoyne's defence. Breymann's death, together with the capture of his grenadiers and the occupation of their defences, meant disaster, for an anchor-post or corner of the British line had been lost. General Burgoyne, who had fought at the centre during the afternoon, and was grey, rumpled and sunken-eyed by nightfall, knew how near he was to catastrophe at day's end on the 7th.

He was 55 years old, large and handsome, strong and resource-ful, but he was nevertheless too old for the kind of exertion and stress he had survived on the 7th, even if his spirit had been wil-ling, which it was not after he took the reports.

Skenesboro was in American hands. A retreat was almost out of the question even if his pride would countenance such an idea. Ahead, so near and yet so far, was Albany. On the evening of the 7th there must have been much doubt that his army could reach it.

One thing was clear; with Breymann's position lost, the Bal-carres position could be overrun come daybreak. A fresh line had to be established, and the only way that could be accomplished was to drop back, re-group, consolidate, and investigate the alternatives to another pitched battle against Gates's great odds.

General Burgoyne passed an order for Balcarres's position to be evacuated. Not until one o'clock on the morning of 8th October did the withdrawal to the heights above the hospital's position get under way. There was no rest for the battered, dirty, dull-eyed troops whose uniforms had not been replaced since Canada, and were hardly presentable this late in the fateful year. Shortly after the last soldier left the vicinity of Freeman's farm, daylight came.

Simon Fraser, dying but conscious, apologised to Fredericka von Riedesel for inconveniencing her, and her three small daughters, by lying in the room they occupied. When he died, John Burgoyne lost the best of his tactical generals, the one who could have best exemplified what was needed when Burgoyne ordered the retreat to Saratoga.

Burgoyne's new position, north of the Great Ravine, gave him an excellent command from the heights. The Americans drifted in and occupied his old position on the 8th, and most bitter for the commander, and for his troops, the enemy inherited Burgoyne's hospital and his wounded. There simply was no way to move them on the British retreat.

The fight was not resumed in the morning as Burgoyne expected it to be. He had ordered the artillery to keep the Americans away, and perhaps the ensuing cannonading accomplished this, because, excluding the ever-present and constantly harassing snipers, the Americans kept at a fair distance, busy at their own work.

But lack of fighting enterprise did not necessarily imply inactivity. General Gates sent 1300 troops under Brigadier John Fellows up the east side of the Hudson towards Batten Kill, to flank Burgoyne. Burgoyne, interpreting this to mean an attack from the rear, undertook a fresh withdrawal towards Saratoga. This movement was begun about nine o'clock in the evening of 8th October, and with his troops marching in two columns, with Alexander Fraser's scouts out ahead, Burgoyne led the way until two o'clock in the morning, when a halt was called to allow the bateaux to catch up, and in fact the march was not resumed until four o'clock the following afternoon, with rain falling, and exhausted men and animals barely able to advance at all. Tents were in the wagons, and when these got bogged down and American snipers took a toll of those who tried to go back and help the emaciated teams, the luggage had to be abandoned, as the hospital with its hundreds of injured had been.

Late in the day, Burgoyne and his ragged army reached the Saratoga heights. The soldiers "had not the strength or inclination to cut wood and make fires, but rather sought sleep in their wet cloaths and on the wet ground, under a heavy rain. . . ."

From the Saratoga heights Burgoyne sent a column of troops and some engineers up the river to build a bridge by which the army might cross over on its withdrawal towards Fort Edward.

The Americans under John Fellows took a position across the river and watched as Burgoyne's men dug in.

Burgoyne's position, previously occupied and partially fortified in mid-September, was excellent for defence, for free play or artillery, and, if attacked, for good use of the bayonet, but, like most fixed positions, was susceptible to surround and siege operations. Nearby was the Philip Schuyler mansion. Burgoyne ordered it burned so that American snipers could not use it.

Meanwhile, General Gates, who did not move out in pursuit of Burgoyne until 10th October, eventually was informed of the British forced marching towards Fort Edward, and, assuming this was Burgoyne's main force, made plans to attack it on 11th October.

At dawn on the 11th, however, Gates's error was discovered by Dan Morgan's riflemen, who moved out early, through a heavy fog, and with the aid of a British deserter, learned that Burgoyne's main force was dead ahead on Saratoga heights. Morgan halted his line, including men of the partisan Nixon, and held a short council. When the fog lifted, looking down on Morgan and Nixon from the heights was a very formidable array of British steel. As the partisans watched, Learned's brigade, also marching up, took a stunning volley from Burgoyne's heights, turned about and fled back the way it had come.

Morgan at once moved west and took a position where he was joined by Learned's survivors, and others, completing an effective enfilade of Burgoyne's position.

There was still one way open for Burgoyne on the 10th. By the 11th Americans had him blocked in all directions save one; the north. He could have attempted a fresh withdrawal by way of Fish Kill – or Fish Creek. Gates was dilatory in closing his surround, but by the 12th he had it completely closed, and John Burgoyne, with his four thousand troops, was in a pocket of rebel Americans 1200 strong, with artillery superiority – and commissary superiority; Burgoyne's supplies were almost entirely in enemy hands. There was very little other than what his men carried with them.

On 12th October Gates's artillery fired on a farmhouse they thought might be Burgoyne's headquarters. Otherwise there was a little of the customary sniping by both sides, and once, when

Burgoyne's scouts bumped into some of Morgan's men in the soggy underbrush to the west, there was a brief little furious fire-fight, but generally, the 10th, 11th, and 12th, were not days notable for fierce combat.

John Burgoyne held a council on 12th October. Present were Generals Hamilton, von Gall, von Riedesel, and William Phillips. This was the second such council. At the first one when defeat had been mentioned Burgoyne had terminated the meeting. This time he listened. Gates, it was said, had in the neighbourhood of 14,000 men. Including guns he had captured at Bemis Heights, he could easily out-bombard the King's army. Also, although Burgoyne's position was excellent defensively, it was tactically untenable, could not be supplied, would not be reinforced, and as Gates grew stronger, might even be over-run.

General von Riedesel – whose wife was supervising a hospital in the cellar of that farmhouse American artillerists thought was British headquarters – said there was only one course still open, excluding capitulation: abandon everything but small arms, individual packets of food, take the women, leave behind the ill, and slip away in the darkness of full night on the west road towards Fort Edward. From there, the army might be able to continue its withdrawal and eventually reach Ticonderoga.

Burgoyne balked, as before. This plan, even though it succeeded, meant the sacrifice of his career and his ambition. He wondered aloud if they ought not to remain at the Saratoga bivouac until, perhaps, relief might arrive. If not from Clinton, then from some other source.

The generals were gloomy about this prospect. The army was already on a starvation diet. What would waiting do?

Burgoyne then suggested his earlier plan again: attack the Americans suddenly with great ferocity, and seek to fight past to Albany. Surprisingly, Generals Phillips and Hamilton agreed with this. Von Riedesel, with passion, demanded to know how, in the name of God, this could work now, when they had fewer than 4000 effectives, when it had failed earlier, when Gates had been weaker, and Burgoyne had had something like 5000 men! Take food for six days, said the baron, abandon all else, and proceed "with the greatest secrecy and caution" to withdraw during the night.

Burgoyne agreed, with great reluctance, and instructed von

Riedesel to make full preparations for an immediate retreat. Later, when the German had already begun the preparations, he was sent an order stating that "The retreat is postponed." No reason was given, and by morning there was no need for an explanation, because Burgoyne's command was so thoroughly encircled it could not have stolen away by night, nor fought clear by day if it had been twice or even three times as strong as it was.

The morning of 13th October dawned cold and damp. American gunners unlimbered while riflemen "swarmed around the little adverse army like birds of prey." Gates's men were again spoiling for a battle; they sensed a victory the like of which no American army had dared hope for until now. In the words of von Riedesel

> Every hour the position of the army grew more critical, and the prospect of salvation grew less and less. There was no place of safety for the baggage; and the ground was covered with dead horses that had either been killed by the enemy's bullets or by exhaustion, as there had been no forage for several days. . . . Even for the wounded, no spot could be found which would afford them a safe shelter – not even, indeed, for so long a time as might suffice for a surgeon to bind up their ghastly wounds. . . . The soldier could not lay down his arms day or night. . . . The sick and wounded would drag themselves along into a quiet corner of the woods and lie down to die on the damp ground.

In the afternoon, the hopelessness became so clear it was not possible for even the most optimistic, or obdurate, royalist to fail to appreciate it. Burgoyne called another council, but this time his officers down to the rank of major were summoned. He told the officers all blame for the army's predicament was entirely his. He also said there was no more than five days' rations at the encampment. He then posed three questions: could a British army of 3,500 combatants enter into capitulation negotiations with an enemy without jeopardising the national honour? Was this now the case of their own army? And, was it possible for the army to capitulate and still retain its honour? The officers concurred on all three questions, although some of the junior commanders would, they claimed, hurl themselves upon the Americans if the Lieutenant General wished it to be done.

One can almost imagine von Riedesel's expression at this kind of talk.

Early in the morning, on 14th October, a drummer in a yellow coat marched forth from the British position, and with American marksmen covering him, he beat for a parley. It was a drizzly, grey day, but then the sun had not appeared for about a week.

At ten o'clock boyish James Wilkinson rode down to the American end of the broken Fish Kill bridge, and was met there by General Burgoyne's secretary and Deputy Adjutant General, Lieutenant Colonel Robert Kingston. Under a blindfold, which was protocol but a little ludicrous, Colonel Kingston was conducted to Gates's headquarters. There, he said Burgoyne knew how much artillery and manpower-superiority Gates had, and was presented with terms of capitulation already drawn up, and escorted back to the bridge.

General Gates's terms were not unfair, but John Burgoyne was not yet convinced surrender was the absolute course. Gates wanted the King's troops to ground their arms within their own camp and march out as prisoners of war. Officers could keep personal effects, should submit to honourable parole, and deliver to the victors all stores, weapons, ammunition and documents.

Burgoyne and his general officers objected strenuously to these terms, and countered with some suggestions of their own, which they said would not be subject to alteration by the Americans. Burgoyne's troops would march to the riverbank, fully armed, and there stack their weapons, by order of their own officers. None of the King's troops were to be termed prisoners, but were to be treated as guests and were to be sent home to Britain on British ships on condition that they did not serve "again in North America during the present contest."

No one in either camp seemed convinced General Gates would accede, but he did, and so quickly that John Burgoyne was certain Gates knew that aid for the British was on the way. He was at least partially correct; Gates had only recently got all the details of Sir Henry Clinton's diversionary foray, and was a little worried.

Burgoyne convened another council of his officers to ask if they thought it too late to break off the negotiations, and was informed that the other generals did, in fact, view any such action as a breach of honour.

Burgoyne had another demand to make: the word 'capitulation' was not to be used in the surrender documents. In its place the word 'convention' was to be used. John Burgoyne's army was a 'convention' of troops, not a beaten army. He tried one last time to sway his generals, but they felt Gates's terms were the most generous obtainable. So did some irate American Congressmen, soldiers, and civilians, when the full terms were publicised, but John Burgoyne, finally convinced there was no other way, agreed to surrender his army, and the official ceremonies were set for Friday, 17th October, 1777, in a large field half a mile from Fish Creek, where a tent was to be set up.

TWENTY

The Capitulation

There were autumn colours over the countryside, the reds as brilliant as those scarlet coats in Burgoyne's gloomy camp, when the sun rose on 17th October.

The ranks were dressed, officers made an inspection as though the troops were shortly to parade, and when the drums rolled British and German soldiers marched unerringly to the river and there, by order of their officers, ground arms, and marched away unburdened by weapons as their bands played.

Of the Americans who witnessed this spectacle, a Brunswicker said, "Not one of them was properly uniformed, but each man had on the clothes in which he goes to the field, to church or to the tavern. But they stood like soldiers, erect, with a military bearing which was subject to little criticism. . . . The people stood so still that we were greatly amazed. Not one fellow made a motion as if to speak to his neighbour; furthermore, nature had formed all the fellows who stood in rank and file, so slender, so handsome, so sinewy, that it was a pleasure to look at them and we were all surprised at the sight of such a finely built people."

The music on this occasion was a mournful, old English air to which a number of songs had been written. One was known as, "When the King Enjoys His Own", but the one meant to be remembered on this notable October day was entitled "The World Turn'd Upside Down". An army of the world's most powerful kingdom was surrendering to a horde of ununiformed beardless boys and hoary grandfathers belonging to a nation no one had really taken seriously — up until this day.

John Burgoyne rode towards the tent in the clearing escorted by James Wilkinson. Gates, "in a plain blue frock", was waiting at the tent. Behind Burgoyne rode his four generals. The

Americans struck up some music of their own. Fifes predominated and the air was "Yankee Doodle Dandy."

In the clearing where the tent stood were a number of American officers, including Dan Morgan in clean buckskins for this
occasion. Horatio Gates mounted his horse and rode ahead.
Where he halted Wilkinson escorted the British officers, and
there made the introductions. John Burgoyne woodenly
removed his hat and in a strong voice announced that "the fortune of war, General Gates, has made me your prisoner." Gates
replied: "I shall ever be ready to testify that it has not been
through any fault of Your Excellency."

Later, near the road where the final ceremonies took place,
John Burgoyne offered General Gates his sword. There, too,
what remained of Burgoyne's army marched into captivity.

The real significance of this historic event was not entirely
clear during the month when it happened, and even after the
actual surrender, for some time, repercussions continued to
spread outward like ripples on the surface of a tranquil pond. For
example, shortly before John Burgoyne's surrender, General
Washington had been beaten at Brandywine and Germantown.
Moreover, the Congress was almost despairing of a formal
alliance with France, although the French had been sending supplies right along, and formal recognition of the new nation was
not forthcoming from any quarter. But, six weeks after the surrender, Charles Gravier, Comte de Vergennes, foreign minister
to Louis XVI received word of the defeat and capture of Lieutenant General Burgoyne and his entire army at Saratoga, and two
days later drew up the document of formal recognition of the
fledgling United States, in open defiance of George III's ambassador to the court of Versailles, Lord Stormont.

France became the United States' ally in war against Great Britain, assuring by this act the Americans' victory and national
sovereignty.

The dark clouds did not vanish from the horizon for the Americans when John Burgoyne surrendered, but a situation that had
been verging on black despair up to that time was allowed to
brighten slightly with new hope.

For the rebels the capitulation was a stupendous, an unprecedented, victory. A British field marshal was captive. In fact two
lieutenant generals, two major generals, three brigadiers, with

their aides and staffs, 299 other commissioned officers of the most
martial nation overseas were captives, not to mention 4,836
enlisted men, 197 musicians, surgeons, subalterns, a number of
women, Tories redskins, Canadians. There were no less than
5000 small arms, 27 fieldpieces, ammunition of all kinds, drums,
banners, everything a British army marched with – but not very
much food.

Later, there was a dispute over 648 cartridge boxes surrendered, obviously not all that were possessed by an army of nearly
5000 men, and this was to have serious consequences.

It was such a triumph as most Americans could scarcely con-
ceive. Congress promoted James Wilkinson to the rank of brigadier general simply for bringing it such a stupendous piece of
news, and went in a body to a nearby church to give thanks.
Horatio Gates was decorated with the Congressional Medal of
Honour, which was as large as a saucer and kept tearing his
tunic, so that he wore it suspended around his neck on a chain.

For nine days since Burgoyne's retreat had begun, the poorly
equipped, badly disciplined and not too-well-supplied amateur
soldiers under General Gates had fought the best soldiers in the
world, Britons and Germans, in openfield combat, and whipped
them regardless of the disparity in numbers. Not only were the
Americans nonplussed, but when news of the disaster reached Sir
Henry Clinton in New York, he recalled the detachments he had
left on the route to Albany, which meant that the King's generals
held only New York, the city and island, Philadelphia, where Sir
William Howe planned to winter in comfort, and Rhode Island.

Burgoyne's defeat prompted the royal garrisons at Crown
Point and Ticonderoga to withdraw to Canada. It also inspired
the commanders in Canada to fear another American invasion.

In Parliament the defeat was hailed by the Opposition with a
"howl of insulting triumph," but generally the unpopularity of
the war only prompted people to bemoan what they considered
inevitable; an alliance between France and the rebelling colonies,
a situation certain to prolong a distasteful contest. But with the
peculiar attraction disaster had always had for Britons, when the
initial lamentations were over a number of villages and cities
raised additional volunteer regiments at their own expense, and
in Scotland noblemen set about enrolling battalions, but with
funds from outside sources. In this manner about 20,000 addition-

al soldiers were made available to the royal armed forces.

On 6th February, 1778, the formal treaty of alliance was signed between France and the United States, despite a warning from Britain. In March, the British ambassador was recalled, France and England were considered at war, and if Burgoyne's defeat had not triggered enough grief for his country, Spain and Holland came into the dispute on the side of the Americans. John Burgoyne's defeat at Saratoga was unequivocally the turning point in the War of the American Rebellion.

The terms of John Burgoyne's capitulation, although never quite overlooked for their liberality, did not initially cause much stir, when the rebels were at the height of their elation over the surrender, but afterwards the Congress as well as most American citizens opposed them quite outspokenly. Clearly, to parole five thousand troops simply meant that, while they could not honourably serve in North America again, there was no law forbidding them to replace other troops in Britain who *could* fight in America. Congress, with no intention of honouring the capitulation term calling for repatriation of Burgoyne's army at an early date, recalled the matter of the 648 cartridge cases. These were obviously not all the cartridge cases possessed by Burgoyne's army, and on the strength of this rather considerable shortage, it was alleged that a breach of the surrender convention had been wilfully undertaken by the British.

This attitude was not entirely popular among the Americans. Even those who opposed repatriation preferred some other means for holding Burgoyne's "convention" army, on the grounds that using the instance of the useless cartridge boxes only made the honour of Congress liable to valid criticism.

Nevertheless, most Americans were opposed to sending Burgoyne's army home to Britain, and Sir William Howe augmented this opposition by turning it into suspicion that Burgoyne's troops would be used again in the war.

Under the terms of capitulation Burgoyne's army was to be repatriated aboard British transports. Sir William, although possessed of adequate shipping, procrastinated. He said he would take the "convention" army aboard British vessels providing the troops were delivered to a port currently in British hands. At once, the Americans denounced this proposal as a subterfuge: Howe wanted Burgoyne's army delivered to a British port in order that it could at once be incorporated into Sir William's army.

Sir Henry Clinton, on orders from his monarch, proposed to ratify the treaty of capitulation and immediately undertake steps to implement the terms, but the Congress, caught unprepared by this move from a fresh quarter, responded lamely, saying it knew nothing of any orders from the King of England concerning the ratification of the Convention, that the whole might be, for all they knew, a forgery. But it was also magnanimously said that if a reputable witness would be produced who could swear he saw the King sign the order, then the Congress would reconsider, otherwise, no one was obliged to take the word of General Sir Henry Clinton.

John Burgoyne then incited the Americans to a fresh outburst of anger. He was justified, but justification unaccompanied by tact at a time when a scarlet coat was anathema on the American eastern and southern seaboards, could scarcely be expected to produce any compassionate overtures.

The "convention" army was taken to Massachusetts, there to be billeted until other plans could be made. In early winter of 1777 Boston was already crowded with American soldiers. In the capitulation terms it was specified that Burgoyne's troops were to be suitably quartered according to rank. This condition scarcely obtained with the Americans, but then they were not as class- or rank-conscious as were Burgoyne's Britons and Germans. Nevertheless, the terms of capitulation guaranteed proper and adequate housing and what the prisoners got was quite different. "It was not unfrequent," related a survivor, "for thirty or forty persons, men, women, and children, to be indiscriminately crowded together in one small open hut, their provisions and firewood on short allowance; a scanty portion of straw their bed; their own blankets their only covering. In the night time those that could lie down, and the many who sat up from the cold, were obliged frequently to rise and shake from them the snow which the wind drifted in at the openings."

Added to this was insult, derogation, scorn, and outright cruelty. In a letter to General Gates dated 14th November 1777, while in a depressed and feverish condition, Burgoyne said that he was sorry he could not report that he and his fellow prisoners were being treated in accordance with the capitulation terms, but as a matter of fact the supreme powers of the state" were unwilling to keep faith, or to even demonstrate the common decency human beings were expected to show one another, and as a result, in General Burgoyne's view, "the publick faith is broke, and we are the immediate sufferers."

This letter reached the Congress, which was already reluctant, and was becoming with General Washington's encouragement, downright unwilling, to repatriate the "convention" army. The letter provided another excuse – if one was really needed – to abrogate the treaty. On 8th January 1778 a Congressional committee said that Burgoyne's allegation "of a breach of the public faith is of a most serious nature, pregnant of alarming consequences", meaning that Burgoyne was probably going to use this charge of a breached treaty as a means for absolving himself and his army from the obligations of the capitulation terms, including the ones having to do with fighting again in America.

As long as this was its attitude Congress, could and did claim that "the convention on the part of the British, had not been strictly complied with," and on this basis formally refused to allow the repatriation – which it did by stating that there would be no embarkation for Britons of Burgoyne's army, until a "distinct and explicit ratification of the convention of Saratoga shall be properly notified by the court of Great Britain to Congress." Later, when William Howe's British transports arrived before Boston, in December, they were not allowed to enter the harbour.

Succinctly, while John Burgoyne and some of his officers were permitted to return to Britain, his soldiers were eventually marched down to Virginia from New England, and remained there as prisoners of war until the capitulation of Lord Cornwallis, in October 1781, ended the War of the American Rebellion.

General Burgoyne was allowed to embark for Britain in May 1778, and prior to departure he was required to ratify the following parole:

I, John Burgoyne, Lieutenant General and Commander in Chief of the British Troops under the restrictions of the Convention of Saratoga, do pledge my faith and sacred honour that I will go from here to Rhode Island where I am to embark for Great Britain; that I will not during my continuance at Rhode Island, or in any other of America, directly or indirectly, hold any communication with, or give intelligence to, any person or persons that may be injurious to the Interest of the United States of America or either of them; and I do further pledge my faith and sacred honour that should the embarkation of the Troops of the Convention of Saratoga be by any means prolonged beyond the time apprehended I will return to America upon demand and due notice given by Congress and will re-deliver myself into the power of The Congress of the United States of America, unless regularly exchanged.

Given under my hand this 2nd day of April, 1778.

J. Burgoyne.
Lt. Genl.

TWENTY-ONE

In the Wake of Adversity

Because Britain had the general particulars of Burgoyne's defeat and surrender several months before the General arrived back in London, everyone who might have had some reason to require a defence, such as Lord George Germain who was responsible for giving Burgoyne his orders, had already taken adequate precautions not to be involved in any unpleasantness. It had been Burgoyne's defeat and surrender, therefore it should also be Burgoyne's shame.

When he reached England in May 1778, one of the General's first acts was to request a court martial. One of his next acts was to visit a physician; he had not been in his customary robust health since roughly the time of his last battle.

Lord George Germain, with disarming courtesy, approved the suggestion of a vindicating enquiry, but at the same time thought it only prudent for John Burgoyne not to see His Majesty, under circumstances that would have been embarrassing for them both.

On 21st May the Judge Advocate General, Charles Gould, notified General Burgoyne that, in accordance with a "Warrant under the King's Royal Signature" five General Officers were to be convened "to examine and inquire into the Causes" of General Burgoyne's failure to bring the rebellious Americans to obedience.

On the next day this meeting was convened, and at once the Court wanted to know upon what stipulation Burgoyne had been released to return home. The General replied in all candour. On 23rd May the Board of General Officers noted that under the circumstances they could do nothing because the General was still honour-bound to hold himself in readiness to return to the United States if the Congress of that country so willed it. On

25th May His Majesty approved of these findings, which of course meant there would be no open and detailed enquiry. In other words, whatever General Burgoyne felt should be revealed such as Howe's abandonment of him, was not to be made public, and all the recrimination that greeted Burgoyne upon his return home was to be borne by him alone.

There was, of course, a logical explanation; what possible good could arise from several generals being branded as incompetent when, in this way, only one general suffered? And subsequently, as was the Crown's prerogative, the blighted general could be quietly recompensed when the fury had died down.

Burgoyne's health remained poor. Shortly before leaving America he had become embroiled in a hearing involving an American officer, Colonel Henley, the fiery-tempered commander in Cambridge, Massachusetts, and during the altercation that arose from their differences, General Burgoyne's health, which had been declining for some time, declined still further. Understandably, then, frustrated by his reception at home, exasperated by the scale on which he was condemned rather than defended by notable men, civilians as well as soldiers, unable to exact public exoneration, and certain that his military career was to end in disgrace, Burgoyne's health remained poor. Men, even those who had not survived the strains that had undermined Burgoyne's health since Saratoga, did not bounce back from adversity at 56 as they had at 26, or even at 36.

On 5th June, General Burgoyne received an interesting letter from the Secretary of War, Lord Barrington: his Majesty thought that Burgoyne's presence in America might help the morale, and instigate better treatment of the troops he had surrendered there. It was probably not very difficult to suspect other hands at work here than the King's. Lord George Germain had managed to stifle the court martial, quite possibly he was now undertaking to get John Burgoyne out of the country as well. There was reason for him to wish Burgoyne beyond recall. By June the recriminations had been heard at length, and thereafter Burgoyne's defenders in high places were notable for a candour that threatened to involve Lord Germain in Burgoyne's disaster. For example, as early as December, the Earl of Shelburne said in the House of Lords, "The operation was intended to be carried out by two Generals in concert with one another, and the ministers sent *positive* orders to one General and *discretionary* orders to the other. . . . Mr Howe goes aboard his ships and gets to the other side of Philadelphia. . . . What is the effect of this want of concert? Burgoyne is surrounded and taken prisoner with his whole army. . . ."

Charles Fox who had earlier branded the entire war as a silly business, said that "A gallant officer [had been] sent like a victim to be slaughtered where his own stock of personal bravery would have earned him laurels if he had not been under the hand of blunderers". And General Burgoyne himself, a measure of confidence restored by these defences, replied on 22nd June to Lord Barrington's suggestion that he voluntarily return to the United States as a prisoner, saying that his physician's prescription was adverse to this, and also, that if he returned it would appear that he and the troops had been abandoned by the British Government. A week later Lord Barrington again wrote, saying His Majesty wished Burgoyne to return to captivity in America.

Burgoyne did not return. In fact his health was good again when Lord Barrington's successor, Charles Jenkinson, wrote in September, that by not obeying His Majesty's earlier order to return to America, Burgoyne was considered as disobedient and neglectful of his duty.

In anger, Burgoyne wrote back saying that "The time in which I am charged with neglect of duty has been employed to vindicate my own honour, the honour of British troops and those of his Majesty's allies, under my late command, from the most base and barbarous aspersions that ever were forged against innocent men by malignity supported by power."

What this scheme of getting him back into American captivity amounted to, he thought, arose from the fact that his enemies – Lord Germain, among others – were "systematically desireous of burying any innocence of their guilt in the prisons of the enemy and of removing . . . my person to the other side of the Atlantic Ocean" in order that a parliamentary investigation could not be successfully undertaken.

Finally, the General said that unless he were accorded a fair hearing, he would feel obliged to resign his military commission, and as soon as this information reached those who saw in it their best course for keeping him from having a court martial hearing, was notified that His Majesty was pleased to accept the resignation, and that of course, now, a court martial was impossible.

Subsequently, Burgoyne wrote a public letter to his political constituents in "the town of Preston," in which he reviewed his career, referred to his enemy, Germain, in an oblique manner, and justified his actions quite well. By this time, too, Burgoyne's general popularity, plus a feeling among many Britons that he was being victimised by the politicians, added considerably to his increasing public favour. It did not hurt him, either, that the war dragged on, and despite British triumphs in America, total victory seemed even more remote by 1779 than it had seemed back in 1776. This was a puzzling situation, but the main consideration was that the war was not popular.

Finally, Burgoyne was able to speak out in the House of Commons. When challenged on his employment of Indians, he replied that this was, in his opinion, an essential evil, and he further truthfully stated that he had refused to sanction the kind of warfare Indians usually made. He also said that the men, like St Luc de la Corne, who had led his Indians, had been without morality and honour.

Altogether, he justified everything, including the burning of the Schuyler mansion, the desertion of troops after Saratoga, his return home, and the fact that although the disastrous campaign had been founded upon his own original plan, it had been so subsequently altered and rendered unworkable, that he had been hamstrung while seeking to implement it.

The House was evidently satisfied, but Burgoyne's Committee was prorogued, so that the findings as well as the evidence upon which these were based was not made public. Burgoyne had lost again.

By now enough time had passed to permit Saratoga, and John Burgoyne, to fade somewhat in the light of larger commitments and greater battles overseas. Finally, in April, 1781, the United States Congress passed a resolution calling for Burgoyne's return, and on 16th April General Washington wrote to the supreme British commander, Sir Henry Clinton, that Burgoyne was absent on parole and that the Americans wanted him back. Washington's letter preceded the end of the war, and one of his most furious battles, by six months, but in April no one in Britain or America knew this, although it can most certainly be said that many wished on both sides for that day to arrive.

Edmund Burke, Burgoyne's friend and defender, wrote to Benjamin Franklin concerning this latest attempt to return Burgoyne to America. It seemed to Burke that someone's "artful management" was behind this demand, and after saying to Doctor Franklin that Burgoyne's country had treated him shabbily, Burke asked: "Shall America, too, call for sacrifices which are still more severe?" He rested his appeal, finally, not to an "Ambassador of America, but to Doctor Franklin the Philosopher, my friend and the lover of his species."

Subsequently, through the negotiations of British and American delegates whose responsibility was to decide how prisoners were to be paroled, it was decreed that John Burgoyne could be freed in exchange for 1047 captured Americans, rank and file, and this exchange was ratified on 9th February 1782, when the war had been over for something like four months, and the Americans had no use whatsoever for a British lieutenant general.

The end had come suddenly. Cornwallis had sustained for eight days the cannonade of over a hundred huge siege guns, and his army, slightly larger than Burgoyne's army had been at Saratoga, 7500 strong, yielded to George Washington's 2500 élite American troops and 4000 Frenchmen.

Meanwhile Sir Henry Clinton, who detested Cornwallis, sat it out in New York again. When the news reached England Lord North exclaimed, "Oh God, it is all over," which was quite correct, even though he also, perhaps perfunctorily, urged a continuance of the conflict "for the maintenance of the integrity of the empire," but in the end he retired. With the change of government, and the bitterness of quitting America in defeat that followed, there was a good bit of altered patronage. The King did not take his army's defeat at all well, but such was the temper of the nation and both Houses, that even the customary sycophants were not eager to support him.

Four years had passed since Saratoga. Many changes had taken place which were directly traceable to that historic defeat.

After Cornwallis's defeat many more changes took place, not the least of which, in the words of G. M. Trevelyan, commenced with Lord North's resignation in March 1782, since when "Britain has never been governed save by a Prime Minister and Cabinet responsible not to the King alone but first and foremost to the independent judgment of the House of Commons."

The defeat in America ended forever the Crown's attempt to regain total and arbitrary power. Perhaps, in those grim days following Cornwallis's fall, not many Britons outside the Commons and Lords were particularly aware of this, but John Burgoyne would have been; even more so when military defeat was followed by the end of the North government. Rockingham swept into power, bringing to prominence many of Burgoyne's old Whig friends.

Vindication came, finally. At 59 years of age, since 1778 out of both uniform and favour, John Burgoyne was offered the appointment of Commander-in-Chief of Ireland. Simultaneously he was made a member of the Privy Council. He had reason to believe he had suffered enough, and could now look forward to some peace of mind. He spent six years in Ireland, and found it a place he did not care much for. In early July, 1782 he received the following letter:

My Dear General,
    The worst news has arrived, Lord Rockingham is no more. We lost him on Monday after the most excruciating sufferings. Do let me see you to-morrow morning, but don't call here tonight, for I wish to conceal the afflicting stroke from the Dutchess until tomorrow. Farewell,

Ever Yours,
Portland.

Lord Shelburne's tenure of office in succession to Rockingham was notable for little, and was also short-lived. Nevertheless under him peace with America was ratified on 30th November 1782, although additional treaties with the other belligerents, France and Spain, were not concluded until the following January. Meanwhile John Burgoyne, removed from both disfavour and the financial embarrassment that followed his resignation from the army, had as a major reason for his wish to leave Ireland a romantic interest in an actress, the opera singer Susan Caulfield, with whom he had reached an understanding some time before. In fact, while Burgoyne was Commander-in-Chief in Ireland, Miss Caulfield bore him a son. He was christened John Fox, in August 1782 at St Anne's church, Soho, and was destined to achieve a great eminence, greater, in fact than the honours of his father: the rank of Field Marshal, and a baronetcy.

In 1784, at 62, General Burgoyne resigned his command in Ireland, at an age, he said, when "the temper finds no terror in the loss of income" which was a noble if not very practical sentiment for an elderly soul with a belated family on the way, but the following year, financially pressed, as usual, the General was appointed to a Royal Committee whose purpose was to assess the national defences. President was the Duke of Richmond. Altogether there were 23 members of the committee, including General Burgoyne and another expatriate from the American adventure, Charles, Lord Cornwallis.

It was Burgoyne's view, not popular at the time among the other army men, that Britain, an island nation, needed fortresses a lot less than she needed an overwhelmingly superior navy. For this, and other views that grated on Lord Cornwallis, his lordship said John Burgoyne was a blockhead.

In 1785 the General's advocacy of his personal views on national defence gained some popularity, but in 1786 when his, and the committee's, views were up for serious consideration before the proper authorities, both were rejected. The General, and the nation, survived.

A few years later, in 1788 when war with Spain over trade in the Orient appeared imminent, the 66-year-old General volunteered to serve, with less than a half dozen years of life left to him. No war occurred, and his offer was not accepted.

The world in which John Burgoyne had played a strong supporting role, had ended about 1781. The great issues with which he had been familiar were history by the time he could devote himself to the homely pursuits of fathering a family, and composing an assortment of writings. He probably missed none of the high moments very much, as he progressed towards his last years; it would have been difficult to recall the great moments without recalling, equally, the humiliations they had led to.

TWENTY-TWO

To the Year 1792

General Burgoyne wrote a number of plays, and while the reviews were commonly divided between good and bad, the test of time relegated Burgoyne's best efforts to limbo, and not altogether because such productions as his *The Maid of the Oaks* were dated – it played at Drury Lane in 1774 – but because it was not exceptional entertainment, even in those times.

Burgoyne's weakness for pen and pencil, the tiresome rhetoric that caused ridicule even in his lifetime were with him as long as he lived. Upon occasion he produced witty and interesting poetry, but generally his writing was too pompous, or too overwhelmingly sententious. Even some of his letters appeared to have been produced as though their author anticipated a re-reading by historians. Burgoyne frequently went to the classics for examples, or emptied the barrel of superlatives. He was rarely content with one word if he could use two, but this was also an affliction of his era, so he cannot be entirely blamed, although he attempted at times to out-do even his own most loquacious contemporaries.

Of *The Maid of the Oaks*, Horace Walpole, who disliked Burgoyne, said the play was "as dull as the author could not help making it", while another critic said that "the greatest compliments are due to the skill and abilities of General Burgoyne on this occasion", meaning Burgoyne's original conception of the play. Burgoyne's *The Lord of the Manor*, a comedy written in collaboration with a friend, achieved good reviews, as did *The Heiress*, probably Burgoyne's most successful production. It ran a full season and was highly praised by most reviewers, and even made its creator a little money.

Burgoyne also undertook to create an adaptation of

Shakespeare's *As You Like It*, making an up-dated musical of it, with "some part of the dialogue left out, but none altered." It took a brave man to attempt this. In John Burgoyne's day Shakespeare was next under God to Englishmen, and perhaps this brazen business of attempting to improve on perfection was the cause of Burgoyne's adaptation dying stillborn. Even so, and notwithstanding the centuries that have passed, some of this work, as well as segments of his other creations, proved that John Burgoyne had talent. Granting that not all readers, spectators, and reviewers, saw merit in the identical enactment or dialogue, perhaps all would have been more willing to, if they knew, when Burgoyne wrote the following lines, he had his late wife in mind.

> Encompassed in an angel's frame,
>   An angel's virtues lay,
> Too soon did heaven assert its claim
>   To call its own away.

Burgoyne also adapted *Richard Coeur de Lion* from French to English. It met with a modest degree of success in London, and was accorded good reviews, but unlike Burgoyne's *The Heiress*, which was put on in France and Germany, and was translated into the languages of those two countries, as well as into Spanish and Italian, *Richard Coeur de Lion* brought its adapter little reward for his efforts, and a fair share of criticism.

Walpole, Burgoyne's lifelong detractor, said that Burgoyne's battles and addresses would be forgotten, but *The Heiress* would endure. Well, Walpole was very often incorrect, and not only about Burgoyne. But *The Heiress* was undoubtedly Burgoyne's best dramatic creation. At least it enjoyed the widest popularity, but the plain fact was that John Burgoyne, the career soldier, was at his best when he was in uniform, for, talent aside, his degree of originality was practically non-existent. Even his success, *The Heiress*, appears to have been an adaptation from a story he had read.

Apart from the theatre, John Burgoyne wrote a great number of speeches, letters, General Orders, admonitions to friends and enemies alike, and the large number of communiqués that alternately aroused ridicule and exasperation in the hearts of those who had to read them.

In an era when all public figures appeared to believe that lofty rhetoric was proof of genius, Burgoyne did his utmost to out-do the best. His grammar was not always above reproach, but at least it was far better than the grammar of his sovereign, George III, who could make even his generals wince upon occasion. It has been said that poets make sorry warriors, but as a general who created one good drama in *The Heiress*, Burgoyne deserved recognition.

One of John Burgoyne's last acts of creative writing was undertaken while he was Commander in Ireland. It was 17 pages long, written in his own hand, and constituted his Last Will and Testament. In its preamble he commented on something he had rarely mentioned before; his religious faith:

> Although it is my intention in the general wording of this Will and Testament to dispense with such form as shall not appear to be necessary to establish the validity of the several desires and bequests, yet I esteem a profession of my religious faith to be a proper introduction to the solemn act I am performing.
>
> I therefore declare that from my youth I have lived, and I trust I shall die, in the fullest conviction and truth of the efficacy of the Gospel dispensation; I esteem it a system immediately from God; and I rely upon merits and the oblation of Jesus Christ, as understood by the Church of England, as the only means of salvation.
>
> During a life too frequently blemished by the indulgence of one predominant passion, it has been a comfort to me to hope that my sensualities have never injured, nor interrupted the peace, of others. Of the greater crimes that originate in the forgetfulness of God, or injustice, or malevolence towards my fellow creatures, my heart is innocent, and upon that ground, though with the deepest consciousness how little my best actions deserve when set against my offences, I commit my soul to the mercy of its Creator.

The diamond that had been his wife's pride, given him by the monarch of Portugal, he left to Lord Derby. Otherwise, because he did not have a very large estate, his bequests went to friends and relatives and consisted mainly of personal mementoes, with the exception of the bequest to "Dear Sue", Miss Susan Caulfield. To her, the mother of four children, three daughters and a son, by the General, he left the substance of his estate, with an injunction for reversion to her son, "John, born in Queen Street,

Soho, about the 25th of July, 1782, for his maintenance and education . . ."

There was one stipulation that could hardly have avoided causing pain to Susan Caulfield, who had loved the General: "Whenever I may happen to die, it is my desire that my body may be interred in the cloisters of Westminster Abbey, as near as may be to the remains of my late inestimable wife, Lady Charlotte Burgoyne."

Not too long after the writing of this Will, the General died. He attended the Little Theatre in the Haymarket on the evening of 3rd August 1792, and although his health had been declining lately, he appeared in good spirits that night. The following day, he became suddenly and seriously ill at his residence in Mayfair, and died before most of his friends even knew he had been stricken. He was 70.

The *Gentleman's Magazine* for August, 1792, carried a brief announcement:

> Died, on the 4th of August, at his house on Hertford Street, Mayfair, the Right Honourable John Burgoyne, a Privy Councillor, Lieutenant General of the Army, Colonel of the 4th Regiment of Foot, M.P. for Preston. and author of the much celebrated comedy entitled *The Heiress*. The regret for his death will be extended and lasting.

Burgoyne had requested a private funeral, and that was what he got. "A lady was . . . present whose convulsive agitation showed her to have that within which passeth show," noted the article in the *Gentleman's Magazine*. The lady was Susan Caulfield.

Lord Derby took in John Burgoyne's son, and must have done a creditable job raising him, because he became Field Marshal John Fox Burgoyne, Bt. He too, had a son, but that young man died at sea without issue, and the male line descending from General Burgoyne died with him.

It was the General's wish that his grave be unmarked, and, for whatever reason, his wish was respected. Later, when others would have marked the grave with his name, no one could by then identify the place. Westminster's Burial Register only noted that John Burgoyne had been interred in the north cloister on 13th August 1792. Ironically the General shared with Benedict

Arnold, an American who had beaten him in battle, the anonymity of a grave in London that no one has ever been able to locate.

John Burgoyne was a vigorous man, a strong campaigner, a forthright politician, a man of conscience and compassion. He possessed wit and poise, elegance and dedication. Of the generals sent to America, John Burgoyne was as good and as bad as the others. Britain did not possess any military geniuses during the period of the American Rebellion, or, if she did, none appeared in North America.

Burgoyne epitomised everything that was considered best in eighteenth-century English gentlemen, and very probably if he had been able to serve together with more dedicated men than William Howe and George Germain, he would have returned from America a hero. Failing this, he might have been able to return with his honour intact, as the brothers Howe did, and as Carleton, Clinton, and even Gage, did.

Nonetheless, John Burgoyne was fondly remembered by his soldiers, and perhaps neither he, nor any other conscientious officer, could have asked for more than that.

Bibliography

The Right Hon. John Burgoyne, General, Statesman, Dramatist, by E. B. De Fonblanque, Macmillan and Company, 1876.
Travels Through the Interior Parts of America, by Thomas Anburey, New York, 1923.
Benedict Arnold, Hero and Traitor, by Lauran Paine, London, 1965.
Gentleman Johnny Burgoyne, by F. J. Hudleston, Indianapolis, 1927.
American Heritage, various volumes, New York, 1955–1970.
Revolution in America, by Bernhard A. Uhlendorf, New Jersey, 1959.
Secret History of the American Revolution, by Carl Van Doren, New York, 1941.
The War of the Revolution, by Christopher Ward, New York, 1952. In two volumes.
Decisive Battles of the U.S.A., by J. F. C. Fuller, New York, 1942.
Philip Skene of Skenesborough, by Doris B. Morton, New York, 1959.

Otherwise, there are available for researchers a number of excellent bulletins from the Fort Ticonderoga Museum, from the various New England historical societies, and from the local societies of historians, such as those to be found in Albany, Saratoga, Montreal, Quebec, Concord, and Philadelphia.

The number of books that mention General Burgoyne appear to defy counting. Some, like *Guns of Burgoyne* by Bruce Lancaster, New York, 1939, and "Horatio Gates" by E. W. Stitt, New York, (*Fort Ticonderoga Bulletin* No. 2 Volume 9,) 1953, are difficult to come by although of considerable merit, and other books, best left nameless, serve only the purpose of confusing researchers. But for anyone seriously interested, the field is wide open. General Burgoyne, win, lose, or draw, seems to have earned the interest of more Americans than Englishmen, judging from the number of his early-day chroniclers in America, or at least earned as many, and while many estimable, and victorious American generals of the Rebellion take a good bit of resurrecting, along with such notable British as William Howe and Henry Clinton, John Burgoyne has stood the test of time very well.

Index